HOW TO RESTORE

Chassis and Monocoque Bodywork

OSPREY
RESTORATION
GUIDE 9

HOW TO RESTORE

Chassis and Monocoque Bodywork

Tommy Sandham

Published in 1985 by Osprey Publishing Limited
12–14 Long Acre, London WC2E 9LP
Member of the George Philip Group

Sole distributors for the USA

Publishers & Wholesalers Inc
Osceola, Wisconsin 54020, USA

British Library Cataloguing in Publication Data

Sandham, Thomas
    How to restore chassis and monocoque bodywork.—
    (Osprey restoration guide; 9)
    1. Automobiles—Bodies—Maintenance and repair
    I. Title
    629.2′6′0288   TL255
ISBN 0–85045–644–4

Editor Tim Parker
Associate Graham Robson

Filmset by Tameside Filmsetting Limited,
Ashton-under-Lyne, Lancashire
Printed by BAS Printers Limited,
Over Wallop, Stockbridge, Hampshire

CONTENTS

Introduction

The original idea for this book goes back a long way. It began in 1966 with a Ford Mk I Cortina which developed some rust problems in the rear chassis. I went out and bought an electric welding set and tried to repair the chassis leg. Needless to say, the result was not too successful. Luckily I was able to ask the advice of a professional welder. He agreed to a swap in which he took my electric set while I got a full set of gas welding equipment.

He gave me valuable lessons on how to weld a chassis. I soon discovered that it is one of the most uncomfortable jobs you can do on a car—unless you have some very high ramps or a pit.

My friendly professional had a small wooden garage where he spent all of his six working days a week welding Ford Anglias, Cortinas, Minis and the infamous BMC 1100s. He had a great method of lifting a car. I well remember how he put part of a railway sleeper into a Ford Anglia boot so that the ends were under the side lips of the boot. He then attached a block and tackle to the sleeper, fixed the other end to the roof of the garage and lifted the unsuspecting Anglia right up! Next he got out his wooden stool and sat under the petrol tank welding in a new chassis leg.

Having learned a great deal of respect for the heat of a welding torch, I would *never*, repeat *never* weld next to a petrol tank without taking precautions. He was lucky. He did it every day, and got away with it!

Anyway, back to my Cortina. I learned the basics of welding and was able to make a repair which satisfied the MOT tester. I kept my gas welding equipment and did lots of work with it. My brother bought a Riley 1.5 and we spent the entire Easter weekend one year welding in a new chassis. That car went on for years and years until its next owner blew up the engine. The chassis was still perfect when he scrapped it.

I have personally tackled everything described in this book. I have had no official training, although I did do a night-school course on welding a number of years ago. That was a great help, and very enjoyable, too.

If I tell you what to do here, you can do it—with a bit of common sense! There are a few golden rules which *must* be followed:

1. Take your time. Never tell anyone it will be ready tomorrow. It never is. Make your estimate and at least treble it!
2. Work safely.
3. Ask yourself: 'Will my repair be as strong as the original?' If the answer is yes, go ahead. If not, think again.

Welding is a technique which you acquire over a period of time. You *do* get better. Similarly, chassis welding takes time to learn, and not everyone can master it. Quite literally, it is a pain in the neck! In the beginning you must be able to make a satisfactory join. This is crucial. Later you will get neater, and after a few years you will be able to make a repair which will be all but invisible under a coat of paint!

I have been working on my current project car for nearly four years. Some of the work I did last year is not nearly as neat as the work I am doing now. With a chassis, only you and the MOT man know what it looks like underneath. It's not like panel-beating where everyone sees your mistakes or lack of skill.

Pick up any workshop manual and it will give detailed instructions about all the mechanical jobs, but it will almost certainly stop dead when it comes to bodywork or chassis. Most bodywork chapters just tell you how to clean and polish your pride and joy and slap on some fibreglass if it rusts. The chassis does not exist, according to workshop manuals!

Back in the mid-1960s I started to look for a book which

would tell me what to do. I never found such a book. I did find books with scraps of information in, and I learned some new and useful techniques, but I never did find a book like this one.

Osprey Publishing wanted a book about main chassis sections but I have not stuck strictly to their brief. My private name for this book was 'Everything you ever wanted to know about chassis repairs, but could never find out.'

When you strip and rebuild an engine, there are only a limited number of things which can go wrong. Body and chassis work is totally different. Each part is dependent on its neighbour. If one is rusty, its neighbour might need replacing too. So I make no apologies for covering many odd items in the book.

I have thoroughly enjoyed writing it and I hope you enjoy reading it, and find it useful. Happy restoring!

Finally, I would like to thank: LMC Panels Ltd for permission to reproduce many of their illustrations; Ford Motor Company for permission to reproduce illustrations from their parts books; Alex van der Heijden for reading the draft and making helpful suggestions; Lionel Chandler of Corsham for original artwork, and Latent Image of Liverpool for photographic services.

All photographs by the author.

Tommy Sandham
September 1985

Chapter 1 | **An overview**

Restoring old cars has, until recently, been looked on as a hobby for the rich enthusiast, who has plenty of time and money to spend on Jaguars, Bentleys, Aston Martins and the like. However, in recent years a new trend has emerged. Cars built in the 1940s, '50s and '60s have become 'collectors' items' and because they were mass-produced, the cost of spare parts has been kept low.

As mass-production techniques became more effective, cars were built in hundreds of thousands, with several well-known models easily topping the magic million. This mass production meant that there was an increase in the number of spare parts kept by dealers. And, because a factory could plan to make huge quantities of the same part, automation led to a low price. All this helps the enthusiast who has acquired one of these cars.

When the initial excitement of owning a new 'second hand' car has died down, the enthusiast begins to discover things about the car. Perhaps a bit of rust on a floor panel has caught his eye. Before long he has the carpet up and discovers the rust is more widespread than he thought. What to do?

Because you only think about your chassis when it starts to rust, we will first have to look at various sources of spare parts. The first stop is, of course, the main dealer.

Main dealers keep a stock of body and chassis parts for most cars still in production and in many cases can produce, over the counter, mechanical parts for cars up to perhaps five years old. Body parts are kept to satisfy the demand for accident and insurance work. When the value of a car starts to fall, it becomes less worthwhile to repair it and this translates into less business for the main dealer.

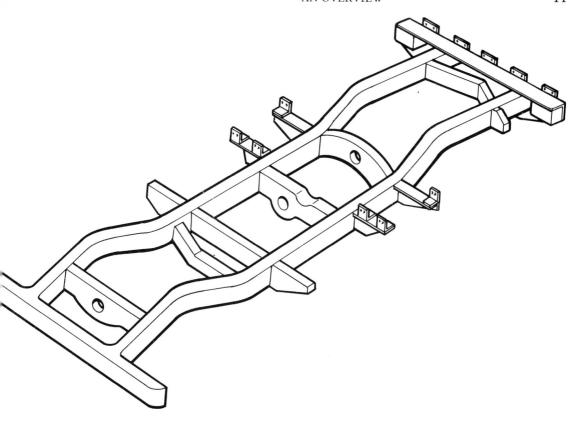

After about five to seven years chassis and body parts seem to dry up.

Panels and repair sections have to be ordered from the factory's central store and although the delay is usually quite short the order can often end up marked 'Out of Stock' or 'No Longer Available'.

Even so, always make the main dealer the first place you visit. Sometimes they have special sales, and they can always check the availability of parts by looking up old parts books. Do not be put off if they are reluctant. Be persistent. Sometimes a main dealer will circulate a list of old or obsolete parts which he has for disposal. Your local dealer may have such a list from another dealer in a nearby town. It pays to make friends with the man behind the parts counter, rather than antagonize him. If he is working *with* you, it is amazing what he can turn up.

This Land Rover chassis shows all the main members and how they are arranged. The body is mounted onto the chassis and secured with bolts. Each outrigger can be replaced if necessary. This construction is typical of a vehicle with a separate chassis

Most of the one-make clubs have regular newsletters. These vary from just a few sheets of paper, to impressive magazines. These newsletters are often the first place to look for wanted chassis parts

Faced with the prospect of no new body or chassis parts being available, the enthusiast becomes worried, because he has previously only dealt with a main dealer. If the main dealer cannot help, what can the restorer do?

If the car was built within the last 25 years and was made in sufficient quantities to be called mass-produced, then the parts *can* still be found. Instead of the main dealers, the enthusiast must now look towards one-make clubs, specialist dealers, replacement part manufacturers, scrap yards and autojumbles. He could always sell the vehicle, but if it needs chassis repairs then the price obtained will be considerably lower than a similar car in good condition. The final choice is to scrap the vehicle. Let's look at the more hopeful choices in more detail!

'One-make clubs', as they are known, cater for owners

of a particular model or make of car. The clubs often have
considerable stocks of spare parts not available anywhere
else and in many cases have started to re-manufacture
essential parts. The best list I know of one-make clubs
appears every second or third month in the UK magazine
Practical Classics. This monthly covers cars built between
1939 and around 1970. Its sister magazine, *The Automobile*
covers vehicles up to 1939 so between them they cater for
all tastes.

These one-make clubs normally charge a yearly
subscription which entitles you to a regular newsletter.
This usually has sections advertising cars for sale, spares
available and other news vital to the owner. It is a sound
investment to join one of these clubs, so make an effort to
find out if there is one for your car. While these clubs can
often help, the enthusiast must also learn to help himself.

Practical Classics **and** *The Automobile* **are simply the best magazines for people who get their hands dirty, rebuilding old cars. Both are published monthly**

He will be given addresses or phone numbers and told to phone up and ask about parts. This is different from what he is used to, and it takes a little time to adapt. However, once he discovers that the people involved in these clubs all share the same interest, our enthusiast will become hooked. He will spend more time on the phone tracking down elusive parts. It all adds to the fun of owning an old car! The next source of parts is the motor factor. Let's have a look at them.

Motor factors and **accessory shops** often have a corner stocked with chassis repair panels, outriggers, sills and so on, and it is always worthwhile asking if there are any parts for your particular vehicle. Motor factors range in size, and could be just a little hole-in-the-wall shop, or a huge modern showroom. Don't despise the little shop. It is incredible what they seem to store in the back room. Well worth asking! The sort of parts we are looking for tend to be made by just a few manufacturers and these people do not seem to advertise very much, so you have to search for them. Remember to ask for a catalogue or brochure when you visit a motor factor's shop. We'll talk more about this later.

Specialist dealers buy old stock from main dealers and other sources and often have hard-to-find items. These

dealers advertise in the magazines, so they are not too difficult to find. These dealers are constantly on the lookout for a main dealer doing a stocktake. Parts which have been lying on a main dealers' shelf for years are not earning any money, and are seen as a nuisance, so periodically the dealers stocktake and clear out. This stock could go to a specialist dealer, or the scrap man. If a specialist dealer takes the parts, he will have to store them as well, so this will be reflected in the price he charges you. But, they *are* available. In one case, an enterprising dealer has started to re-import parts which were sent out to Australia and North America, from the UK, in the sixties.

Sometimes the specialist dealer will undertake an exchange service on some mechanical parts and will also be able to advise you about body or chassis parts. Often there is a well-known modification which can save you a lot of time and money. For example, a part from another car may fit your vehicle. It is certainly worth a phone call to find out what the dealer can do for you. Look out for these dealers at autojumbles too, which brings us to the next subject.

Autojumbles seem to be getting more popular and come in all shapes and sizes. (I have even heard of smaller ones being called 'boot sales' where the participants sell parts from the boot of their car!) The bigger ones range

Above left **Make the main dealer your first stop for spare parts. Even 20–25 year old cars might still have parts available**

Above **Don't despise the small motor factors. This little shop has an incredible stock of spare parts hidden away**

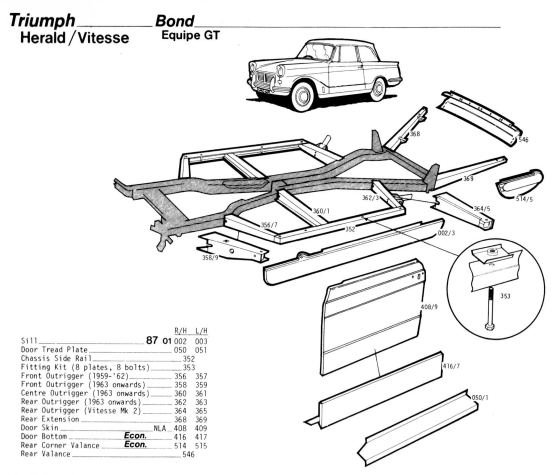

Triumph _____ **Bond** _____
Herald /Vitesse   Equipe GT

	R/H	L/H
Sill _____ **87 01**	002	003
Door Tread Plate _____	050	051
Chassis Side Rail _____		352
Fitting Kit (8 plates, 8 bolts) _____		353
Front Outrigger (1959-'62) _____	356	357
Front Outrigger (1963 onwards) _____	358	359
Centre Outrigger (1963 onwards) ____	360	361
Rear Outrigger (1963 onwards) _____	362	363
Rear Outrigger (Vitesse Mk 2) _____	364	365
Rear Extension _____	368	369
Door Skin _____ NLA _	408	409
Door Bottom _____ **Econ.**	416	417
Rear Corner Valance ___ **Econ.**	514	515
Rear Valance _____		546

The Triumph Herald has a separate chassis and the body really should be removed to do any serious repair work on it. (Reproduced by permission of LMC Panels)

from just a few stalls at a country show or traction engine rally, to massive two-day extravaganzas with hundreds of stalls. Normally, anyone can rent a stall for a fee and fill it with used spares. Costs depend on the size of the event. It pays to have a really good look round these meetings as you always find something interesting, such as spares, tools, manuals handbooks—or just inspiration. It is also useful to ask around if you do not see what you want. In this way you can find useful addresses and phone numbers. It really is quite amazing what you can turn up! It is also a great day out for the family.

Scrap yards are not really a day out for all the family. Traditionally, they consist of a muddy field with lots of crashed cars, but some are now making an effort to be tidy. They dismantle the car and put the spares on a shelf and you buy over the counter. However, they do not normally interest the enthusiast who is looking for older parts which our new generation breaker will not have.

The traditional breaker's yard is still a major source of spares. Although you may have only ever bought mechanical spares, is there any reason why you should not buy second-hand chassis parts? The same rules for choosing mechanical parts apply to choosing chassis parts. Is the part worn, damaged, rusted or otherwise unsafe? If the answer is no, you should buy it. Later in the book we will describe how to recover a chassis part from a scrapper and what to do with it. Another useful service which scrap yards can provide is to show enthusiasts the difference between several so-called identical vehicles. This does not often happen with chassis parts, but can happen with other parts which concern us in this book, such as cross-members, mounting brackets and so on. Keep your eyes

The good old Ford Anglia has many useful parts available so don't send yours to the breaker's yard just yet! (Reproduced by permission of LMC Panels)

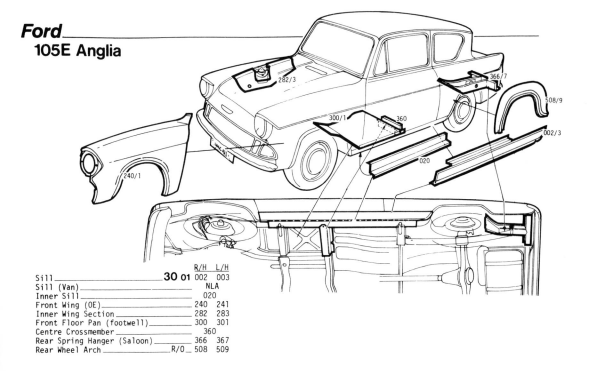

Ford
105E Anglia

		R/H	L/H
Sill	30 01	002	003
Sill (Van)		NLA	
Inner Sill		020	
Front Wing (OE)		240	241
Inner Wing Section		282	283
Front Floor Pan (footwell)		300	301
Centre Crossmember		360	
Rear Spring Hanger (Saloon)		366	367
Rear Wheel Arch	R/O	508	509

1100/1300 — *MG* —— *Riley* ————— *Vanden Plas* —— *Wolseley*
1100/1300 Kestrel 1100/1300 Princess 1100/1300 1100/1300

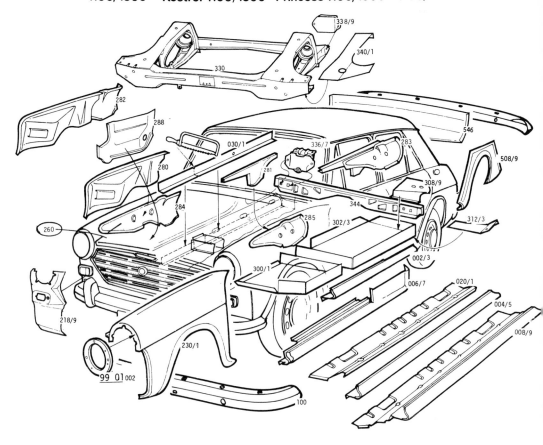

	R/H	L/H
Sill (full length - 2 door)__**08 06**	002	003
Sill (full length - 4 door)_____	004	005
Sill/Lower Side Panel (2 door)__R/O_	006	007
Combined Sill and Floor Panel_____	008	009
Under Sill (closing panel)_____	020	021
Interior Sill (floor angle)_____	030	031
Front Bumper_____		100
Rear Bumper(Not Mk 2)_____		140
Front Panel Corner (Mk 2) *Econ.* R/O_	218	219
Front Wing_____	230	231
Headlamp Ring_____99 01_		002
Bonnet_____R/O_		260
Inner Front Wing (top) R/H_____	280	
Inner Front Wing (top) L/H_____		281
Comb. Inner F/Wing & Trumpet R/H___	282	
Comb. Inner F/Wing & Trumpet L/H____		283

	R/H	L/H
Inner Front Wing Trumpet R/H _____	284	
Inner Front Wing Trumpet L/H _____		285
R/H Inner Front Wing (lower) _____	288	
Front Floor Pan (Footwell) _____	300	301
Rear Floor Pan (Footwell) _____	302	303
Rear Under Seat Panel _____	308	309
Rear Under Floor Section _____	312	313
Rear Subframe _____		330
Rear S/frame Mount Rubber (front)___	336	337
Rear S/frame Mount Rubber (rear)____	338	339
Rear Subframe Repair Plate _____	340	341
Rear Subframe Mount Panel _____		344
Rear Wheel Arch _____	508	509
Rear Valance _____		546

open when you visit a yard. And, when you go on holiday you can hunt out the yards in your holiday area.

Remember too, that the stock in a scrap yard changes quickly. One year there are dozens of one model, the next year they have entirely disappeared. So make sure you make the most of any opportunities.

Advertising for the required part will often work wonders, as enthusiasts are always keen to help each other out. Here again, one-make clubs often have a list of parts wanted and for sale. Also, have a look through the classified adverts in your local papers. Lots of interesting items turn up here, especially in the 'Under a Tenner' columns. I once advertised for a manual, and ended up with a manual, a parts book and a tea-chest full of spares! Another time it took me six months to locate a rear crossmember for my 1963 Ford Capri. The more effort you put into finding a spare, the more chances of success and the more fun it is!

If you have tried everything and still cannot find the part you want, you can either:

1. Scrap the car if the missing part is vital, such as a Ministry of Transport (MOT) test part. (This is the British safety test requirement. Other countries may or may not have such a test.)
2. Have a part specially made and fitted.
3. Make the part and carry out the repair yourself.

Let's examine these choices in a bit more detail.

The first choice, scrapping the vehicle, is definitely the

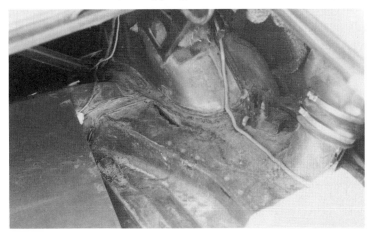

Far left **I won't make any comment about 1100s, but aren't there a lot of parts available for them? (Reproduced by permission of LMC Panels)**

Left **The owner soon discovers things wrong with his new secondhand car. Perhaps a rusty hole in the floor, or in the boot as in this example. This can easily be patched**

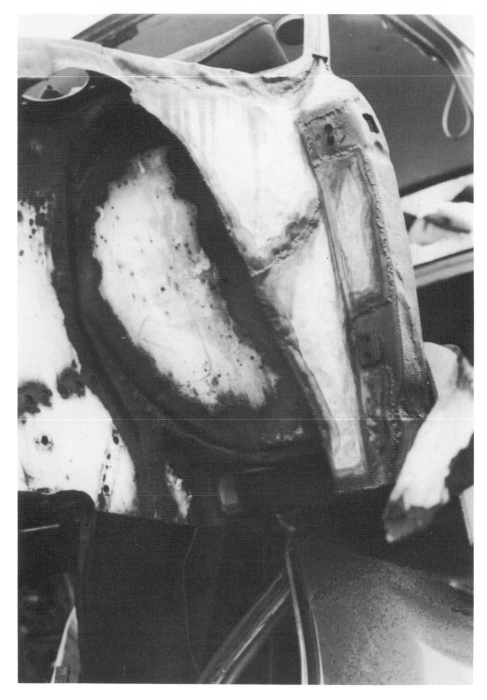

last resort. Once it has gone you cannot bring it back. A lot of work goes into a car and it is always worth one last effort to keep it. Of course some cars get so dilapidated that the only safe place for them is the breaker's yard. You could always advertise your faded classic in the one-make club magazine as 'breaking for spares'. This will help other people and improve your cash-flow too! You will probably make more breaking a car yourself than selling it to a breaker. However, having broken a number of cars over the years, I find that the biggest problem is what to do with all the bits that are left over. Surprisingly little is actually sold; the rest you have to dispose of. You *must* consider this carefully before you break a car.

The second choice, having a part specially made could cost a lot of money. If you decide to put the job in the hands of a professional—*beware!* There are all sorts of people offering all sorts of services and at all sorts of prices. Ask around before giving work to anyone. This may seem obvious but it is only after a job is badly done that you have time to regret your action. A good professional can work wonders on a car body or chassis. Pick a good man and be prepared to pay for his services.

Then there is the third choice. This is what this book is about. Do the work yourself! You have many advantages over the professional. You have unlimited time to spend on the job and unlimited supplies of sheet steel which is relatively cheap. You should also have the ability to get the job right.

The terrible words, 'You've got a rotten chassis, mate!' strike fear into the hearts of most motorists, who immediately think of expensive welding and endless weeks off the road. For the enthusiast with an older car there are extra problems, as fewer and fewer garages want to get involved with an obsolete motor car. But provided you have some basic skills and are prepared to learn, you *can* do substantial repairs in the home workshop.

The first thing to do is to explore the extent of the rust or damage. This is covered more fully, later in the book. The main point to remember is that in a unit construction car, one component of the chassis affects several others. So it is no good, for example, replacing a rusty crossmember and

Know your limitations. This brave attempt at rebuilding a Ford Anglia ended in the breaker's yard. The complete door post has been fabricated from new steel

trying to weld it to a rotten floor section.

Most of the work depends on your ability to weld. There is an extensive chapter about welding later in the book, and you should also read Bob Smith's *Sheet Metal Bodywork* in this Osprey series.

You will need to find out if your car has a separate chassis, where you have to remove the body to do a proper restoration job. Cars such as the Triumph Herald, the MGA or the Jaguar XK150 have a separate chassis, but it might be possible to do limited repairs on this type of vehicle without removing the body. This would have to be very carefully done to be satisfactory. Remember too, that heat from the welding torch could still reach the floorpan, even though the chassis is bolted to the floorpan, so you must take all the precautions outlined later in this book.

Unit construction cars have fewer problems when you come to line up a replacement part. There are three reference points for each part. For example, an outrigger is welded to the outer sill, to a main chassis rail, and to the floor. This gives you three reference points, and any error will be minor. I have never had any problems with this subject. Follow the golden rule: cut out one section at a time, weld in the new, then go on to the next section.

With separate chassis cars you will have to take much more care to locate a repair part, prior to welding. The official factory manual usually gives reference points so that accurate measurements can be taken of a chassis. Use these to help locate the new part.

In this book you will be shown how to tackle different jobs. Do not consider them as the only ways. Professionals have different methods, special tools and so on, and even they would disagree on how to do a particular job.

Here you are offered instructions and as much practical help as possible. With a little care and practice you can carry out quite advanced work. Throughout the job, ask yourself this simple question, 'Will my repair be as strong as the original?' If the answer is yes, continue. If not, think again.

Here are ten rules to guide your chassis restoration:
1. Work safely.
2. Don't bodge—the repair could last 25 years.

3. Remove one section at a time.
4. Do not try to burn off paint with the welding torch.
5. Grind steel down to bare metal.
6. Don't turn the lit torch on the hoses.
7. Clamp the parts together.
8. Tack weld first.
9. Do a bit at a time.
10. Paint when you have finished welding—not the next day.

Below left Unless it is very important to save this vehicle, it should be scrapped. Holes in several floor sections plus corrosion in the chassis outriggers spells a lot of work

Below On an otherwise fairly sound car, a new chassis outrigger can be welded in cheaply. The outrigger will cost little but you will need paint and underseal to protect the job

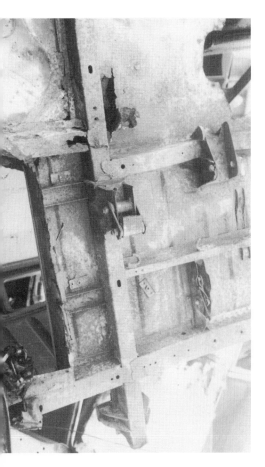

Chapter 2 | What is available to the restorer?

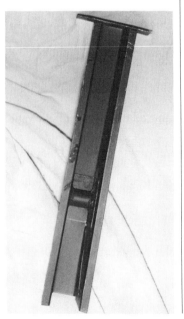

This is a Mk I Ford Cortina saloon rear chassis leg. With some modifications it became a front outrigger on the author's car. It cost a lot less than the real part and was much easier to find

Before we start to get our hands dirty, let's settle down and have a look at what is available to chassis restorers, and the tools they need to put rusty ones to rights. Let's be quite clear though—this book does not attempt to give you guidance on repairing accident damage. All we are dealing with here is rust damage. If your chassis has suffered accident damage, you must seek expert help.

In this chapter, I want to try to emphasise some of the problems you will encounter when you start substantial chassis repairs. It can be a very dirty and unpleasant job, first when lying on the ground chiselling off lumps of rusty chassis, then when trying to weld in new steel. Your shoulders and neck will ache with the unaccustomed strain of holding a hammer and a welding torch. And, if you do not take precautions, your eyes, hair and skin could all suffer damage or injury.

So don't rush out and start chiselling. Make another cup of coffee and read the rest of this book. I want to describe what sort of things you will find under your car, what sort of snags you will stumble on, and how to avoid cuts, bruises and burns.

First, we will deal with tools. If you were asked what tools a panelbeater needed, you would quite confidently answer, 'hammer, dolly, body file, mallet' and so on. If you were then asked what tools a chassis restorer needs, you might well be stuck for an answer.

Let me allow you to rummage through my toolbox. It will probably surprise you, and at the same time give you a better idea of what is useful. But remember, a professional might have quite a different set of tools.

First of all I *do* use a proper panel beating hammer. Mine

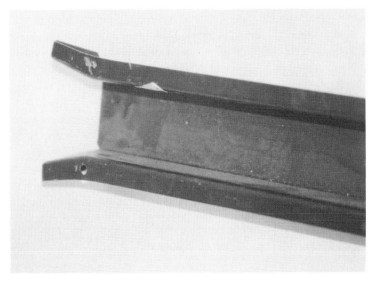

Above **This lower, inner sill has been patched, but I don't think you will see it. The front outrigger supported by the jack is the modified rear chassis leg**

Left **A close-up of the end of the outrigger. The ends are splayed outwards to provide a stronger location to the outer sill. The hole is a left-over from the manufacturing process**

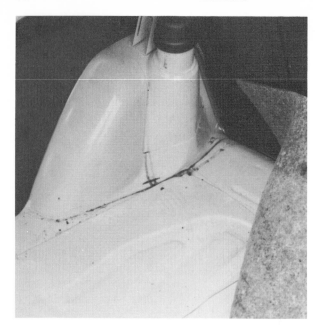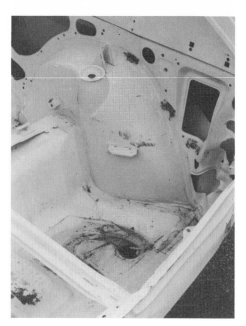

Above right **The inner wheelarch
on an almost-new bodyshell. The
lines of sealer show where the
various panels meet**

Above **With just 10,000 miles on
the clock, this new car is already
showing signs of rust round the
rear wheelarch join. The carpet
was wet too, indicating a leak.
This will need immediate
attention, otherwise you will be
welding in a new floor panel and
wheelarch before long**

is a Sykes-Pickavant 560 standard bumping hammer and it
came as a birthday present. It was not expensive. I *only* use
this for dressing the edges of chassis legs, floor pans and
anywhere else there is a clean edge. I *never* use it to hammer
welds. If you are not quite sure what 'dressing' means with
reference to panel work, it means to straighten an edge or
lip. You usually dress a piece of metal by holding a dolly
block on one side of it and striking the other side of the
metal with a hammer. This straightens out any lumps or
ridges.

If I did more chassis work I would probably want a pein
and finish hammer. There are several of these in the Sykes
Pickavant catalogue, but the one I have my eye on is
number 565. I would use the pein face for stretching metal,
when I form a curved surface such as when making a
valance.

Dolly blocks, or dollies as they are more usually
described are discussed next. I have about four dollies
now, but I only find one or two of these really useful. I seem
to use one of them all the time. It is called a toe dolly and
has a Sykes-Pickavant number 550. It weighs about 3 lb

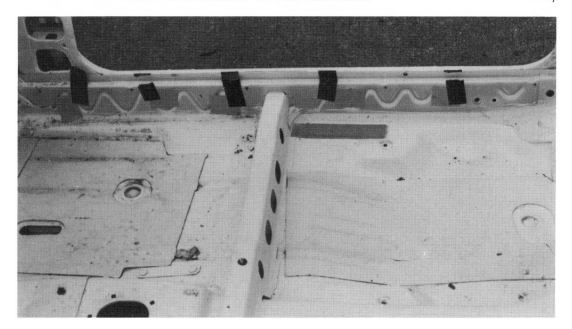

and has several different faces which can be used for different jobs.

Once again, if I did more chassis work, I would want a dolly with a groove down it, known as a shrinking dolly. This is used to sink welds and can also be used in conjunction with a hammer to put grooves into metal. This will be discussed later.

All dollies should be kept rust-free and the best way to do this is to keep them in an old oily sock!

These are the only 'proper' tools I use. The rest are borrowed and adapted from other trades. For example, I often use a bricklayer's hammer which has a long spike on it. The bricklayer uses the spike to split bricks, but I find it is perfect for getting into tight corners where an ordinary hammer will not go. Be careful if you use this type of hammer. You can easily hit yourself in the face with the spike if you use the normal face. It can get a bit confined under a car.

I have a 2 lb hammer which I usually use with my 4-inch chisel. This combination is good for removing rusty chassis legs and floor panels. Be sure to keep your chisel

While older unit construction cars had most of their outriggers and chassis strengthening parts outside, later models have the same parts inside. This shows the centre crossmember on a modern saloon

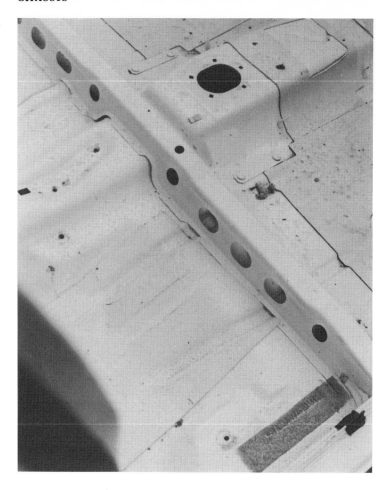

Above **Another view of the
centre crossmember showing the
lips welded to the floor panels. If
you turn the photo upside down,
you will have a very clear idea
of what you will meet under an
older car**

Right **A basic 'top hat' shape (to
the left) with the shaded area
showing how it can be modified
to produce the (right) shape. All
outriggers and many chassis
members are made from this
basic shape**

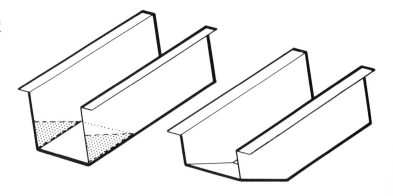

sharp. You might ask why I do not use a 4 lb hammer. It is because when you are lying on the ground, chiselling above your head, a 4 lb hammer is much too heavy to hold.

I use a small, joiner's staple hammer which has had its head ground away at an angle. I bought it that way from a garage sale—it is useful for dressing welds and all sorts of other dirty jobs. I use it a lot with my shoe-maker's last.

I got the shoe-maker's last at a jumble sale several years ago. The last is used as an anvil, but I have ground a groove in one face and I use this part of the last to put strengthening grooves in sheet steel. More about this in a later chapter.

I also have a joddler (or joggler) which is used to set a small edge in sheet metal. This allows you to overlap two pieces of metal without a lump showing at the join. Although this tool does a good job, I find that I do not use it very often.

Also in the toolbox is a 4-inch angle grinder, (you can get by with just a Black & Decker drill—I did for years!) This is a very versatile tool and needs some discussion.

Always wear goggles. My angle grinder turns at some 10,500 rpm, and at this sort of speed, precautions are necessary.

If you are lying under a car grinding welds, make sure that the shield on the grinder is turned to give you the maximum protection. You will find that the sparks given off will hit you on the face, so take care and think which way the sparks will go before switching on. These little sparks are red hot and can do a lot of damage. They will embed themselves in glass and cannot be removed. I have damaged a windscreen in this way—so be very careful of these sparks.

The machine can also be used as a cutter by fitting a cutting wheel. Again, take care to use the correct wheel for cutting steel. A wide cut is made, so bear this in mind when planning each cut.

A wire cup brush is also available and this makes short work of removing rust, loose paint and so on. Make sure you buy the correct wire brush, as if it is not built to revolve at 10,500 rpm it could easily disintegrate.

I have spent some time discussing the angle grinder

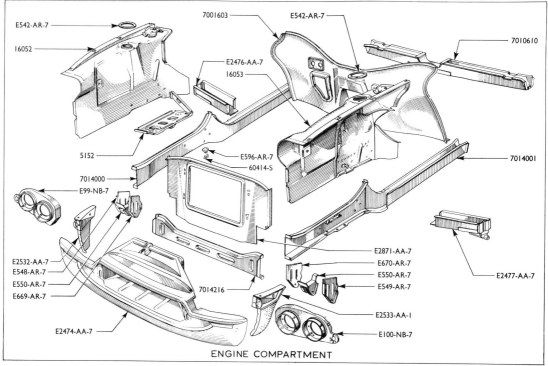

ENGINE COMPARTMENT

Taken from an official Ford Motor Company parts book, the following drawings illustrate the typical construction of a sixties car

because it is such a versatile tool. You can use an ordinary drill instead, which turns at about 3000 rpm, but once you have used an angle grinder, you will never want to go back. It is a dangerous tool, so be very careful when using it.

Back to my toolbox. It includes a hand drill, a rubber mallet, and an assortment of clamps. You cannot have too many clamps. They also make great Christmas presents. I have about six different kinds of clamps, but always seem to need more.

Lots of different types of clamp are available, and they all do the same thing. They allow sheets of steel to be held tightly together, prior to welding. They all have a very powerful lever action, are adjustable over a wide range, and will stay in place until they are released by unlocking them.

One useful device worthy of special mention is a little screw clamp which allows another clamp to be made into a small vice. This makes a lot of jobs easier and the clamp can be attached to any suitable place such as a fence post or an old chair.

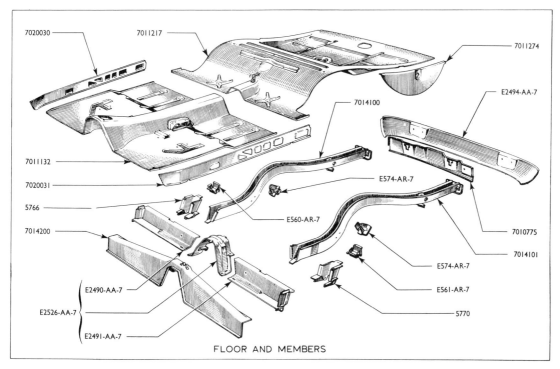

7020030
7011217
7011274
E2494-AA-7
7014100
7011132
7020031
E574-AR-7
5766
E560-AR-7
7010775
7014200
7014101
E574-AR-7
E2490-AA-7
E2526-AA-7
E561-AR-7
E2491-AA-7
5770

FLOOR AND MEMBERS

While we have been discussing the 'Mole' type of clamp, we have overlooked the old favourite the 'C' clamp. This uses a screw thread to tighten the two faces which hold things together. The only problem with C clamps is their throat depth—that is the distance between the backbone of the clamp and the clamping surfaces. You can never have it deep enough. No matter what you need to do, you will find that the throat depth is not enough. They are still useful, though. They come in all sorts of sizes, from tiny little things, right up to what are called joiner's sash cramps. (A joiner uses them to hold frames together while building tables and other large items of furniture.) You might be able to pick up a set in a jumble sale, although they can be quite expensive items.

A strong pair of pliers is useful for removing sharp pieces of scrap metal. They can save many cut fingers, as it is a great temptation to try to break off little bits of metal left over when you break a spot weld. Resist this temptation, and always use pliers.

Ignore the part numbers, but notice how many parts make up the chassis/floor unit

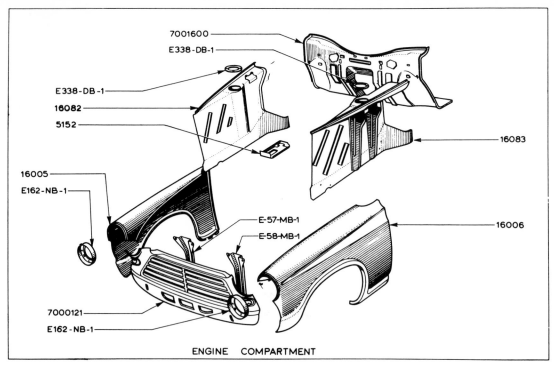

7001600
E338-DB-1
E338-DB-1
16082
5152
16083
16005
E162-NB-1
E-57-MB-1
E-58-MB-1
16006
7000121
E162-NB-1

ENGINE   COMPARTMENT

Moving up front, the inner wings locate onto the main chassis rails, forming the fourth side of the box section

I have several pairs of tin-snips which are used to cut sheet metal. You can get right-handed snips and left-handed ones. They are not 'handed' for the owner, but for the side that the waste metal leaves the snips. This can be quite important sometimes. Right handed snips coil the waste on the left side of the blades. Left-handed snips coil the waste to the right. In both cases the steel being cut is left free from distortion. Snips can be used on metal up to about 16 gauge. If you want to cut anything heavier, use a hacksaw. If you get a chance have a look at both right-handed and left-handed snips. If you can afford it, you should buy both, but you can manage quite well with just one pair.

Finally I have a hacksaw, a junior hacksaw, a steel rule and a few files. A pop rivet tool is also useful.

Another useful tool for cutting steel is the 'Monodex' cutter. This needs just a small pilot hole drilled in the steel, after which the small blade is inserted into the hole and the cut is started. They are useful if you cannot get good access

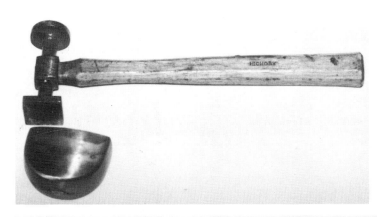

Left **The professional's body working tools, the panel beating hammer and dolly. If you own a good hammer like this, look after it and do not use it to strike welds if you want to keep it smooth**

Below **These are just three types of clamp which are available to the restorer. They come in all sorts of shapes and sizes, but I find the one on the right most useful**

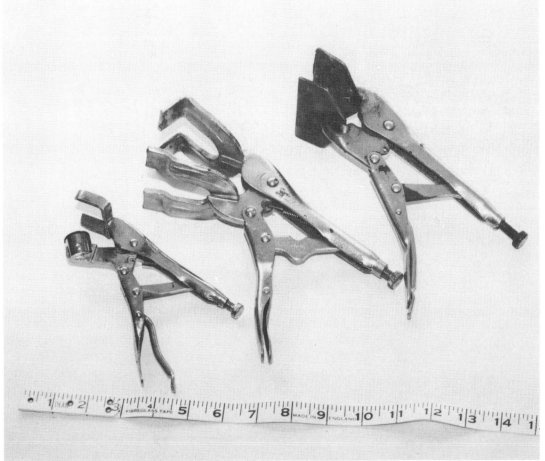

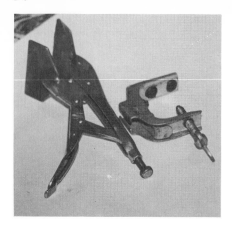

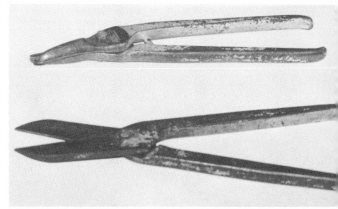

Above **You can buy this handy little clamp which clips to the bigger clamp to form a useful vice. You just have to fasten the clamp to a handy chair or fence post**

Above right **Two different snips. The snips in the forefront are straight-cut while the pair behind are 'handed' snips as described in the text**

Right **A (Black & Decker) 4 in. angle grinder. Very effective in use, it needs to be treated with great respect. It can be fitted with grinding discs, cutting discs or wire brushes. The wire brushes do not last long due to the speed of rotation**

to the panel to be cut. For example, if you had to open up a chassis member to get to the inside, you would use this type of tool. They come into their own when a circular cut has to be made, such as when making a MacPherson strut repair panel. This is discussed later in the book.

If you want to punch a nice neat hole, try a tool borrowed from the radio industry. It is called a chassis punch and was originally used to cut nice round holes in radio chassis, so that valves could be mounted. They come in sizes from about 10 mm to 31 mm and from $\frac{3}{8}$ in. up to $1\frac{3}{8}$ in. You may be able to find larger ones. The idea is that you drill a small pilot hole at the centre of where you want the big hole to be. Next, one half of the punch is placed above the steel, the other half below. The two halves are pulled together by a

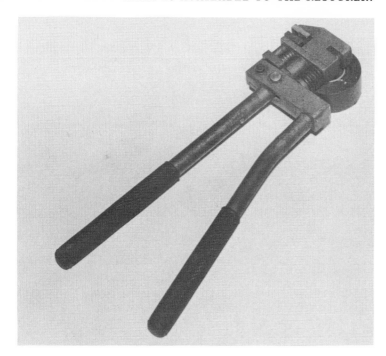

Left **This tool is variously known as a joggler or joddler. It puts a step on the edge of a sheet of steel, so that another piece can overlap without leaving a ridge. Useful when making up the edges of inner sills**

Below **A close-up of the head of the joddler. This type has two heads, one which makes the edge and the other which punches a nice neat hole in thin steel. These holes are ideal for spot or plug welding**

A bit rough and ready maybe, but the good old hammer and chisel cannot be beaten for removing old rusty chassis parts. Don't overdo things though—just a bit at a time

screw which runs through the pilot hole. Slowly but surely a nice neat hole is cut. Have a look at the accompanying photographs to see how this is done.

The last time I saw chassis punches advertised, they were low priced, depending on the size. Try a radio spares shop.

You are going to need at least one pair of axle stands and a strong jack. Try to get a really tall pair of stands, as every extra inch you can raise the car makes the welding job so much easier. Remember, though, that to get the car to the height of these tall stands you will need a jack which can lift to that height. Alternatively, be prepared to lift the car in two stages. Get it as high as the jack will take it, then support it on a stand. Let the jack down and place some strong timber between the jack and the car. This time you will gain extra height depending on the thickness of timber. This procedure, like all work on a car, should be carried out with great care.

A set of ramps could be handy if you can afford them, but I would go for the axle stands if money is tight.

Similarly, although a hydraulic jack is nice, a strong screw or scissor type will do just as well. Incidentally, don't overload a jack. Either it is designed to lift a heavy machine or it isn't. Don't take chances.

Welding is normally done with gas equipment, and the British Oxygen Company (BOC) Portapac is excellent for the job. You can often hire this equipment from DIY hire shops, but ensure that it is working properly before you take it home. Welding is fully described later in the book.

In case you are starting to think that this collection is highly specialized and costs a lot of money, let me reassure you. It has taken a number of years to arrive at this assembly of tools—some 15 years in fact—and on the way I have worked on about a dozen cars. You can quite easily make do with just a few items, but remember to keep your eyes open at the autojumbles!

Now let's have a look at some of the chassis repair parts which are available, before we start to make our own. This might be a suitable time to tell you not to use old railway lines or bits of battleships to patch up cars. The 'thin' steel used in the original chassis is quite strong enough if properly welded in. Don't try to 'add extra strength' as it only ends in disaster!

A number of specialists make and supply chassis and body repair parts. These parts are supplied for the most popular cars, so while practically everything exists for a Mini (or a Chevrolet), there are fewer parts for the more exotic cars. However, if you are restoring an ex-works rally Mini Cooper 'S', remember it uses the same body and chassis parts as Granny's shopping car. Similarly, a 1200 cc Ford Cortina has the same chassis as a 135 bhp Cortina–Lotus. However, when I chose to restore a 1963 Ford Capri, I had to make most of my repair sections!

The best way to find out what is available is to browse through all the car magazines you can find and make a note of any likely addresses. Send off for price lists and catalogues and when you get them, file them safely in a plastic wallet. What you are now building up is a valuable reference library of chassis parts. This will become more and more valuable as the years pass. In ten years' time, when parts are even harder to find, you will know what *was* available, which makes the job of looking for it, or making it, that much simpler. Incidentally, if you make an effort to collect catalogues like this, never throw them away.

If you cannot find the chassis parts you want straight

My converted shoe-maker's last. The top face has a nice smooth groove in it which puts a useful shape into sheet metal. I often use it to strengthen small metal parts

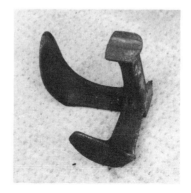

away, do not despair. Parts from another car or another model from the same factory can be adapted. Let me give you an example.

At one time I could not find a replacement front chassis outrigger for my 1963 Ford Cortina Mk 1. The outrigger also serves as a jacking point so it has to be very strong. While trying to locate a suitable donor part, I noticed the Cortina saloon rear chassis leg in a catalogue. I ordered a new part and measured it. I found that it was a few inches longer than the outrigger I wanted, but the other dimensions were very similar.

The next problem was the jacking point. If the rear leg had only been a U-channel it would not have been strong enough and would have required considerable modification. However, the Cortina rear leg has reinforcement already welded in—where the rear spring mounting is located. The Cortina jack locates with a small stub on top of a flat plate. The stub locates in a hole in the chassis outrigger. All I had to do was drill a suitable hole in the chassis leg. As luck would have it, where I wanted to drill my hole was in the heavily reinforced area. So the transplant looked very satisfactory.

An old pair of leather gloves can save many a cut or burn. The tyre lever on the right is used as a slapper, to form bends in steel. The vicious-looking hammer is supposed to be used by bricklayers, but I find it useful for reaching into tight corners. Take care with that spike, though

The 'new' outrigger also needed to be shortened, so this was done, leaving $\frac{1}{4}$ in. lips at either end to weld to the inner sill and main chassis member. The rear leg cost me around £5. A similar idea could save your car from the breaker's yard. (It is fair to tell you that later on I discovered the correct part was still available, but it took a lot of finding and cost more than three times as much as my adapted one).

A three-sided chassis section like this is often referred to as 'top hat' and the reason will become obvious if you look at some of the photographs. Although this is quite strong in its own right, it becomes much, much stronger when a fourth side is added. The fourth side is made up from the floor panel. This makes a square section which is very light and strong.

The chassis designer uses different lengths and sections of these three-sided members to build up a chassis. It might be as well to spend a little time now and see how this type of car is actually built in the factory.

The body and underpan is fabricated from lots of different panels. These panels are brought together in the assembly area and are spot welded together. The parts are held in precision-built jigs which ensure that they are fitted together correctly. Despite this, the finished car can be up to $\frac{1}{4}$ in. 'out' if all the tolerances in the dimensions were added up. No one would ever know unless the chassis was carefully measured against its body drawing, perhaps after an accident.

The panels to be joined will be put in the jig by an assembly line worker, or by a robot. Various grooves and flanges will ensure that they are correctly located. At this stage the steel is unpainted, to aid the spot welding procedure.

The spot welder is then positioned so that each electrode is on one side of the metal to be joined. Where two surfaces are to be joined they are fitted tightly together in the jig. The spot welder operator then presses the electrodes onto the metal surface and presses the ON button. A strong electric current is passed from one electrode, through both sheets of metal to the other electrode. This current heats the area of metal through which it passes. The electrodes

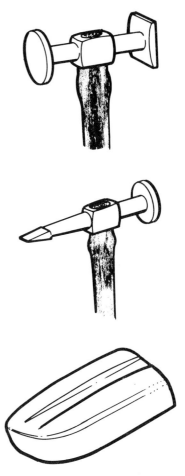

Top **the standard bumping hammer, well known to panel-beaters.** Above centre **is a pein and finish hammer used when stretching metal.** Above **the dolly is a shrinking dolly, used to put grooves in sheet metal**

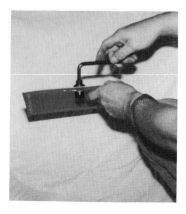

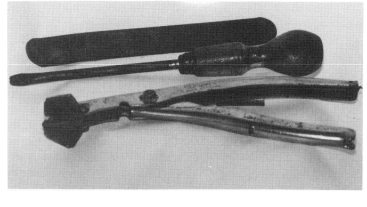

Above **The chassis punch in action after a pilot hole has been drilled. Turning the Allen key brings the two halves of the punch together to make the hole**

Above right **The tyre lever has already been described. The big screwdriver is great for forcing between spot welds while the Monodex sheet metal cutter is useful where you only have access to one side of the metal**

are normally about $\frac{1}{4}$ in. diameter and produce a spot weld between $\frac{1}{8}$ to $\frac{1}{4}$ in. across.

This local heating increases until both sheets of metal start to melt under the electrodes. After a pre-determined time (calculated after numerous tests) the current is switched off and the two electrodes are removed from the surface of the steel. The result is a strong spot weld which will have totally penetrated, and fused, both sheets of steel. The spot welder operator will then move the electrodes along the surface a little way and repeat the process. In this way the chassis is fabricated. Once a reasonable number of sections have been put together, the chassis is put onto the assembly line and the rest of the car is built onto it. The process, being highly mechanized, lends itself to automation and robots. The only parts requiring maintenance are the electrodes. They have to be cleaned and re-set after a certain number of operations.

This spot welding process has a number of advantages over other processes; the heating is local, and there is little distortion. The weld is neat and does not need any finishing work. (Other welding techniques may require grinding or other finishing). The process can be carried out quickly and repeatedly. In this way the car body/chassis is fabricated. But after what could be a very short time, these sections begin to rust, resulting in our enthusiast having to learn how to repair them.

Let's move on now to another chapter, and get down to the real work—making or adapting chassis parts.

Chapter 3 | How to make your own parts

Another angle on 'top hat'. Armed with a few lengths of this, the enthusiast can restore almost any chassis with the help of gas welding equipment

In these pages I will try to pass on to you as much information as I can. You may find that there is too much information, or—if you have done this type of work before—you might think there is not enough.

The problem in writing a book of this sort is trying to decide the level of the reader's expertise. I have tried to tell you things you will need to know. Chassis repair and chassis welding still has a certain mystique about it, in the same way that welding did, up until quite recently. Now, every practical motoring magazine is offering dozens of home welding kits. I shudder to think at some of the repairs which are being done with this equipment. At least it must be keeping the MOT tester busy!

Some of this new generation welding equipment looks quite useful. Others look downright useless. I have advocated the use of gas welding equipment in this book as there is, quite simply, nothing to beat it, and it is so versatile. Try heating a stubborn nut with an argon arc set!

The repairs that you do now, could last another 20–30 years or more, if proper rust-proofing treatment is carried out. Do not be tempted to take short cuts to save a day. What is one day out of 20 years?

Work safely at all times and always ask the question, 'Will my repair be as strong as the original?'

After reading this book, you can always answer, 'Yes!'

We have seen that a lot of chassis repair parts are available, but you might find that the vital part for your car is not available. Do not worry too much. Later on, there are instructions for removing chassis parts from a scrap car. If you cannot find even a secondhand part you will have to make your own. But before cutting any metal for a repair

Two examples of chassis parts made from the basic 'top hat' shape. In the front of the picture is an outrigger, while the part behind is a rear chassis leg, complete with reinforced spring mountings

job it pays to spend a bit of time looking at the job and planning how to tackle it. If it is a rusty chassis outrigger which has to be replaced, its position in the chassis and its relationship with other parts will have to be examined.

If the old part is removed, will the chassis be seriously weakened until the new part is welded in? Does removing the part present any particular problem? What preparation work must be done on the other side of the floor to which the chassis attaches? Remember too, that if you have to replace the outer sill for example, you might find that the inner sill needs to be repaired. And if you have luck like mine, you will find that the inner sill needs attention where it connects to an outrigger. So—from just one part needing repair, we suddenly have three to be tackled.

As an example, let's look at the process of measuring a rusty outrigger and the first steps in constructing a new one. (It might be worth pointing out that I use both the terms 'chassis legs' or 'outriggers'. There does not seem to be any hard and fast rule about this, so let's decide that an outrigger runs across the car, while a chassis leg runs in the fore-and-aft direction of the car).

Before considering the gauge (or thickness) of the metal used, determine where the part begins and ends. Normally chassis outriggers will run from the main chassis to the inner sill (or side member) and will be some 12 to 18 in.

long. Lips on the ends of the outrigger will overlap the main chassis and these lips are used to weld the two parts together. In the factory the parts will have been spot-welded together, as we have already seen, but to make the repair the restorer should normally use a gas flame.

Having discovered the general shape of the outrigger, your next step is to measure it, either with a steel rule or a steel tape. If a rule is not convenient, a $\frac{1}{16}$ in. diameter welding rod can often be used to match the length of the outrigger with the excess rod bent out of the way. A measurement can then be taken from the rod and put down on paper, in the form of a drawing or plan.

The important dimensions are length, width and height—forget about metal thickness for the moment. Add about $\frac{1}{4}$ in. to each end of your drawing for each lip. So if your outrigger is 14 in. long your drawing will be $14\frac{1}{2}$ in. The lip size is generally $\frac{1}{4}$ in., but a little more will be acceptable. Anything less makes things very difficult when it comes to welding, so aim for at least $\frac{1}{4}$ in. Take a bit of time over this drawing and try to get it accurate.

Next, draw the shape out on paper. Use dotted lines to show where the metal will be folded. When you are happy with the measurements and the shape, cut out a paper shape and try it for size against the original chassis. Do not worry if it is a little too big—you can always trim paper! If it is too small you have done something wrong, so start again.

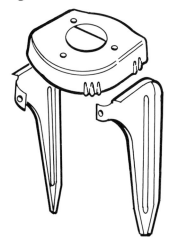

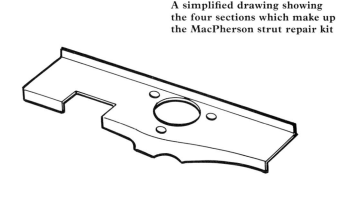

A simplified drawing showing the four sections which make up the MacPherson strut repair kit

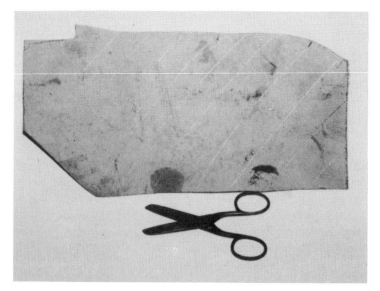

Right **A do-it-yourself template kit. An old piece of cardboard, a pair of scissors and a pencil are all you need to make your own templates**

Below **Just a few of the templates which I have used recently. The ones marked RH were used to make the corners of a rear valance, while 'R/H wing' are part of another repair job on a front wing**

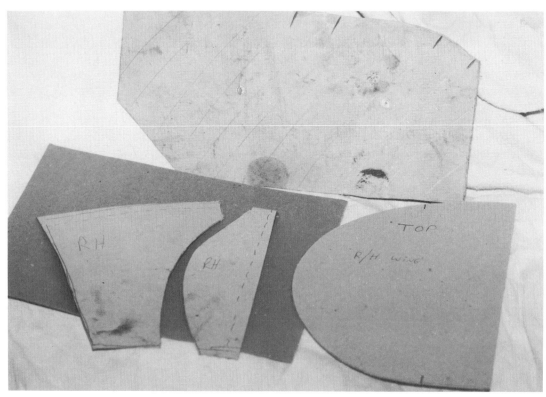

If there are any holes in the outrigger, for example drain holes or a hole for a jack to locate, these will have to be accommodated in the drawing. Mark their locations with a big blob. Jacking points normally have to be reinforced, and this reinforcement will have to be built in to the new part. We will consider jacking points later on.

Will it be as strong as the original? Yes, if you follow the guidance given here, and the welding is satisfactory.

Having completed the paper shape, and when you are happy with it, the next step is to transfer the shape onto cardboard. You might ask, why not make the template in card straight away? Well, if you are like me, you will get it wrong first time round—paper is much easier to work, and cheaper to use. The cardboard will become your working template (unless you want to make a wood template, if you think you might be doing the same job again in the future) and will be used to mark out the metal. Check that the cardboard shape fits the shape of the original part, as a mistake at this stage could cost you several hours of work.

When you are satisfied that the cardboard shape correctly fits the shape of the original outrigger, it is time to consider the material and its thickness.

There are several thicknesses of mild steel used in the construction of a car chassis. For most of the items needing real strength, such as box sections, the top hat is pressed from 16 or 18 gauge (1.6 mm and 1.2 mm). Occasionally, where extra strength is needed 14 gauge (2 mm) might be used. The gauge of steel works in reverse to the thickness. The higher the gauge number, the thinner the steel. So 12 gauge is heavy while 20 gauge is much lighter.

Over the years outer panels have become thinner. The designers say it is because the monocoque construction is stronger, but others will tell you that it is done to keep costs down. Either way, a wing is normally pressed from 20 or 22 gauge (1 mm and 0.8 mm). One by-product of thinner wings (apart from rust) is that they cannot easily be beaten back into shape in the same way that a heavy, prewar wing can. The idea is that if it is damaged, it should be replaced. This theory is fine until the car becomes obsolete. Then the parts still rust out and become even harder to replace. This is known as built-in obsolescence!

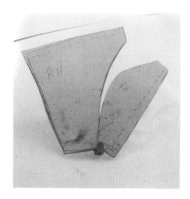

Held together for the photograph, these two cardboard shapes form a compound curve when cut out of steel and welded together

Above **This Mini floor has had some professional attention. Unfortunately, while the patch is neat and the welding good, the original rusty steel is underneath. Within a few weeks water was seeping in through the original hole underneath**

Right **Bits from battleships. This van has had a new floor welded in. It looks like armour plating but must have done the job for a time. It would have been better to buy a new floor section**

To help you 'mix and match' I have measured a number of sections from well-known manufacturers and listed them in a table. All you have to do is select the part closest to the one you need and decide if you can adapt it. All the information needed to adapt a part like that is contained in this book. There is a list of manufacturers making chassis parts at the back of the book.

Above **New sill held on by clamps. At this stage you should stop and check that everything lines up** and **that the door will still open and close!**

Left **A shiny new sheet of steel ready to be made into repair sections**

These Chassis sections are available from dealers:

Depth	Width
1 in.	$\times$ 2 in.
$1\frac{1}{2}$	$\times$ 1
$1\frac{1}{2}$	$\times$ $2\frac{1}{4}$
$1\frac{1}{2}$	$\times$ $2\frac{1}{2}$
$1\frac{3}{4}$	$\times$ $2\frac{1}{4}$
2	$\times$ $1\frac{1}{2}$
2	$\times$ 2
2	$\times$ $2\frac{1}{2}$
2	$\times$ 3
$2\frac{1}{4}$	$\times$ $1\frac{1}{2}$
$2\frac{1}{4}$	$\times$ 2
$2\frac{1}{4}$	$\times$ $2\frac{1}{4}$
$2\frac{1}{2}$	$\times$ $1\frac{1}{2}$
$2\frac{1}{2}$	$\times$ 2
$2\frac{1}{2}$	$\times$ $2\frac{1}{2}$
$2\frac{1}{2}$	$\times$ 3
$2\frac{3}{4}$	$\times$ $2\frac{3}{4}$
3	$\times$ $1\frac{1}{2}$
3	$\times$ 2
3	$\times$ 3
$3\frac{1}{4}$	$\times$ $3\frac{1}{4}$
$3\frac{1}{2}$	$\times$ $2\frac{1}{2}$
$3\frac{3}{4}$	$\times$ $3\frac{3}{4}$
4	$\times$ 2
4	$\times$ 3

These sections are all available in lengths of about 4 feet. You can buy sheets of steel from motor factors. The sheets come in sizes from 3 ft × 3 ft up to 6 ft × 3 ft. Now you know about sheet steel and top hat sections. The only section I have not told you about is the angle section. This is normally 90 degrees, or a right angle. It comes in the following sizes:

$$1 \text{ in.} \times 1 \text{ in.}$$
$$1\frac{1}{2} \times \frac{1}{2}$$
$$1\frac{1}{2} \times 1\frac{1}{2}$$
$$2 \quad \times 1\frac{1}{2}$$
$$2 \quad \times 2$$
$$2\frac{1}{2} \times \frac{1}{2}$$
$$2\frac{1}{2} \times 2$$
$$3 \quad \times 1\frac{1}{2}$$
$$3 \quad \times 3$$
$$3\frac{1}{2} \times 2\frac{1}{2}$$
$$4 \quad \times 2$$
$$6 \quad \times \frac{1}{2}$$
$$9 \quad \times \frac{1}{2}$$

These all come in lengths of about 4 ft. As a rough estimate, you will probably pay about £1 per foot for these sections—more for the sizes with bigger sides!

Now that you know what is available, I am going to tell you how to fabricate a piece of 'top hat' from a flat sheet of steel. You will only need to do this if you cannot find exactly what you are looking for, but it is handy to know how to do it anyway. You will use the same techniques for making up odd repair patches and panels.

The first job is to measure the thickness of the original piece of chassis. Use either a wire gauge or a micrometer. It is very difficult trying to measure very thin, rusty steel with a ruler!

Having selected the gauge of steel to be used for the repair panel, lay the cardboard template on top of the steel and scribe the shape onto the metal. You can use a proper scriber bought from a tool store, but an old screwdriver sharpened to a point will do just as well. A pencil could be used but the line gets rubbed off too easily, while a marker pen line is usually too thick.

Mark the lines to be folded with dotted or broken lines. With the final shape marked out on the sheet steel, cut out

Sheet Steel

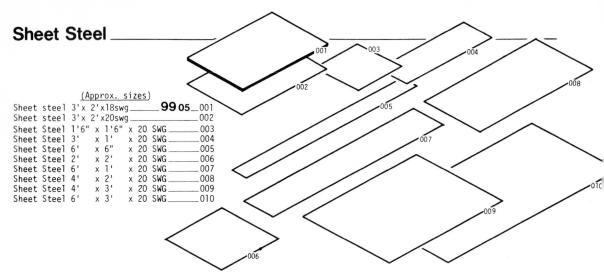

(Approx. sizes)

Sheet steel 3' x 2' x18swg	**99 05** 001
Sheet steel 3' x 2' x20swg	002
Sheet Steel 1'6" x 1'6" x 20 SWG	003
Sheet Steel 3' x 1' x 20 SWG	004
Sheet Steel 6' x 6" x 20 SWG	005
Sheet Steel 2' x 2' x 20 SWG	006
Sheet Steel 6' x 1' x 20 SWG	007
Sheet Steel 4' x 2' x 20 SWG	008
Sheet Steel 4' x 3' x 20 SWG	009
Sheet Steel 6' x 3' x 20 SWG	010

Chassis Channel

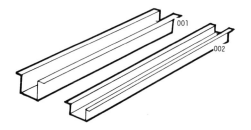

(Approx. sizes)

Chassis Channel 36" x 2¼" deep x 2¼" wide	**99 10** 001
Chassis Channel 36" x 1⅝" deep x 2⅛" wide	002

Angle Section

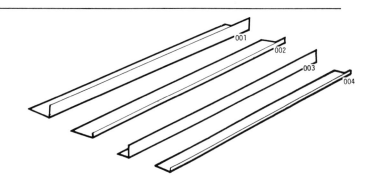

(Approx. sizes)

Angle Section 60" x 3" x 2"	**99 15** 001
Angle Section 60" x 3¼" x ¾"	002
Angle Section 60" x 1¼" x 1½"	003
Angle Section 60" x 2½" x ½"	004

the shape using either tin-snips or one of the other cutting tools described earlier. You now have a flat piece of steel which, when bent, will become your new chassis outrigger.

In industry, metal bending machines perform miracles in a few seconds. Not just right-angled bends either. A skilled operator with a suitable machine can produce all sorts of curves, angles and folds. The enthusiast is more limited, but can still produce useful bends in the home workshop.

For accurate bending, a fixed piece of steel, such as a

Far left A selection of steel sections and sheets available for home restoration. (Reproduced by permission of LMC Panels)

Above **The rear end piece for this sill has been made up and welded in place. The wheelarch needs some more work, and you can see where the end piece has been left ready to meet the new wheelarch**

Above **A view to bring despair to the faint hearted! However, this old sill has been chiselled off to reveal the inner sill in very good condition making less work for the restorer**

Right **This is the original front piece for my sill. The next illustration shows my template to make a new end piece. Don't throw anything away until the job is complete!**

length of angle iron, is a must. In some cases you can use a suitable length of wood as a former.

To bend your outrigger:

1. Place the piece of metal in a vice, with a strong piece of wood or angle iron aligned with one of the folding lines marked on the metal.

2. Normally the longest bend is done first. With the vice done up tight, so that there is no chance of the metal moving about, strike the metal as closely as possible to the bend line, using a rubber mallet, or a slapper and hammer. A slapper is simply a flat piece of metal. I use an old tyre lever for this job. The slapper helps to spread the load and prevents the sheet metal being marked by the hammer.

   The metal is struck as close to the bend line as possible, in order to reduce the chances of a bend forming in the wrong place. (If the metal was struck too far from the required bend line and at the wrong angle, a bend would begin to form in the wrong place).

3. Having started the bend, check that the metal is still aligned properly and that the bend is following the required line.

4. Continue to strike the metal until the bend becomes near to a right angle. If angle iron is used as a former the angle of the bend can be judged from the visible leg of the angle iron. After a check to see that the bending line has not moved, strike the metal until a nice, tight, right-angled bend is formed. Take the metal from the vice.

   The second bend is more difficult. Be careful to follow the instructions, or you will end up with a 'Z' instead of a 'U'—you only need a 'Z' for a Morgan side member!

5. Place the metal in the vice with the shorter, folded, side to the bottom. It will be seen that when the former is aligned with the second folding line that the jaws will not shut without fouling the first fold. The answer is to 'pack' the space between the jaws with a piece of wood, so that the jaws can be tightened sufficiently to allow the second bend to be made.

6. Align the second fold line with the angle-iron and with

the packing piece in position, clamp it up tight.

7. Make the second bend in the same way as the first one.

You should now have a piece of metal bent into a 'U' shape. In order to form the lips a further packing piece of wood is required. It must fit exactly beween the two walls of the U. Clamp the U in the vice with the packing piece in place and the angle iron in line with the bending line for the lips. Tap the lips over with a hammer.

Turn the outrigger round and form the lips on the other side.

The lips on the end still have to be formed but to do this a number of small hacksaw cuts have to be made. It will be seen that in order to allow the ends of the walls of the U to be bent outwards, a small cut has to be made at the top and bottom. This can be done with a hacksaw or tin-snips and it should be $\frac{1}{4}$ in. deep. The bend can now be made by holding the outrigger in one hand and tapping the lip over while held against a vice. Repeat the process for the other end.

You will now be left with a little tag of metal at the top of the U and at each end. This can now be cut off. Finally, to complete the job and give it that professional finish, each sharp corner should either be smoothed with a file, or cut with tin-snips.

You could go along to a local sheet metal shop instead. Simply make an accurate measurement of the chassis leg and make a rough drawing with all the dimensions and take it to the sheet metal shop. They will fold steel to almost any shape you care to show them (including curves, so you can have sills made quite cheaply). The last time I had this done, I got two 3-foot lengths for next to nothing.

Make sure your measurements are accurate or you will run into problems matching the new section with the old. Lips have to be bent at each end of the section where it is welded onto the next part of the chassis and these lips need to be about $\frac{1}{4}$ in. wide.

If the outrigger needs to be welded before offering it up to the vehicle, this should only be done after a trial fitting.

If the outrigger you need is not straight, it might be simpler to buy the top hat with the same measurements as the required outrigger, and cut a section out of the wall to make the new shape. The bottom of the outrigger would then be bent up to meet the wall and seam welded into place. The drawing shows what to do.

Floor panels

There are two types of floor panels. The first type is a small pressing which might consist of a single foot well. It can be bought from a repair panel dealer, complete and ready to weld in.

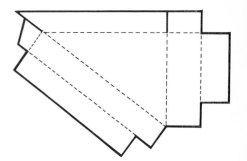

My sketch for the new end piece, tidied up by an artist. The dotted lines are for folds

The second type of floor panel is much larger, in some cases it is a complete floor pan containing both passenger and driver side floorwells and part of the transmission tunnel. You could buy a new one of these but might run the risk of having the car fold up when you cut the old one out. It makes better sense for the restorer to repair this type of panel.

An example of the smaller type of floor panel is the BL Mini floor pan. The larger type is used on the Cortina series of Fords. It consists of the complete floor pan plus the transmission tunnel.

If an area of floor is to be replaced, do not restrict yourself to a small area. There are many occasions when it is actually easier to replace a larger section of floor rather than just welding on a small patch.

Remember, if you decide to cut a floor section from a scrap car, also to take the sound deadening pads and any grommets which might be missing from your car. You can always take grommets from the other piece of floor in the scrap car.

Floors tend to rust from the top down. This is due to soggy carpets holding in the water. How many times have you ever dried out your carpet and underfelt? Leaks are caused by faulty rubber seals or from holes in the wheelarches or spare wheel well.

To repair a floor panel:

1. Buy the new panel or cut the required part from a scrap car. Make sure you get the correct pan for the model year and version of your car. More important still, make sure you get the correct side. You are going to look a bit of a fool standing with the driver's side cut out and a

passenger side floor pan in your hand!

2. Measure the new pan against the original floor.

3. Remove the seat, carpets, underfelt, sound deadening pads etc. If you cut corners you are inviting trouble when you light up the welding torch!

4. See if you can find the original seam where the panel joins its neighbour. You may have to remove some paint, perhaps with a wire brush in the electric drill.

5. Mark out the area to be removed—with chalk, or pencil. Check underneath the car for fuel lines, brake pipes, cables and wiring. If there are any they will have to be removed, or protected in some way.

6. When you are sure that the new panel will fit correctly, either cut away the old panel with hammer and chisel or, if you are not going to use the complete replacement panel, cut away the required area.

7. Remove the old panel but leave a few small lips to help locate the new part. These lips are simply little projections, left when the panel is cut out. They provide support for the new panel to rest on, prior to welding. They can be welded in afterwards, or ground away.

8. Dress the edges of the floor with the hammer and dolly and remove paint with paint remover, a grinder, file or wire brush.

9. Place the new panel into the space left by the old. You may find it easier to push the panel *up* from beneath rather than down from the top. It depends on the car and the panel.

10. The panel can be held *up* by a jack, or down on the lips which you left in step 7.

11. When it is in place and you are happy with it, tack weld the panel into place. This involves welding the new floor to the body in half a dozen places.

12. When you have again checked that the fit is correct, weld all round. To help reduce distortion do a few inches on one side, then a bit on the other. Every so often, stop welding and dress the welds with the hammer and dolly. (*Not* with your good panel hammer!)

13. Finish welding all round and complete the dressing with hammer and dolly.

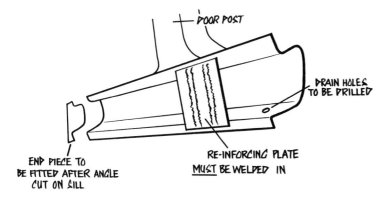

DOOR POST

DRAIN HOLES
TO BE DRILLED

END PIECE TO
BE FITTED AFTER ANGLE
CUT ON SILL

RE-INFORCING PLATE
MUST BE WELDED IN

Above **Another sketch showing the general construction of a sill which I wanted made in a sheet metal shop**

Left **This is the steel shape which the local sheet metal shop folded for me. I then added the front and rear pieces and welded in the reinforcing plate shown in the sketch above**

Replacing sills

There are some golden rules which apply when working on sills. These are:

1. Only work on one sill at a time.
2. Support the rest of the car as the sill provides a lot of strength. Use axle stands and jacks. *Do not use bricks.* (Bricks have been known to actually explode under the concentrated weight of a car.)
3. Match the new sill against the old sill *before* cutting any steel. Make sure you have been sold the correct sill or that you know what modifications have to be done, to make the sill fit correctly. When you are completely happy about the sill, carry on. Measure the gap between

the bottom of the door and the sill for reference. You will need this measurement when you fit the new sill.

4. Chisel off the old sill.
5. Inspect the inner sill and all edges where the sill meets the floor, door pillar, etc. and where the sill meets the rear wheelarch. Allow plenty of time to do this work if you must make an estimate.
6. Repair any damage to any of the above surfaces.
7. If you then paint or protect the inner surface of the sill against future rust damage, it pays off in the long run. Use a proprietary rust prevention compound. Finally, finish off with a nice thick layer of underseal. Remember some of it will burn off during welding but you can always apply some more through suitable holes.
8. Locate the new sill in place with clamps, pop rivets or Mole Grips. Use as many clamps as possible. Only when you are absolutely sure that the sill is correctly located, go on to the next step.
9. Tack weld the sill into place. This involves welding the sill to the body every three or four inches. Do not be tempted to braze. If you have welding equipment, then *always* weld. When you have tacked the sill in place, remove the clamps and try to open and close the door. Now is the time to decide that the sill does or does not fit. Check the gap between the bottom of the door and the sill. Take any corrective action required now, not later.
10. When you are satisfied that the sill is fitted correctly, weld the rest of the sill in place. There may be extra work involved where the sill meets the rear wheelarch, but you should have worked this out when you prepared the job.
11. When welding is complete, grind down any visible welds, to tidy up the job.
12. Undercoat the sill as soon as you finish welding, otherwise it will immediately start to rust.

MacPherson strut repairs
One of the most common repair jobs on a modern car is either to weld a sheet of steel over a rusty outrigger, or to weld a patch on top of the MacPherson strut tower.

Let's look at the MacPherson strut repair first, because I want to spend more time on general patching later.

The MacPherson strut is now fitted to lots of cars but for some years it was identified with European Fords. When the British MOT test was introduced, it became common for Fords to be failed because of severe corrosion at the top of the strut mounting. The specialist dealers were quick to spot this and they produced a repair patch. At first it was thought that you could get away with merely pop-riveting this patch in place, but this idea was quickly quashed. It had to be welded in place. Patching this area must be done with care. There is no point in putting a new repair panel on top of the already rusty steel. This is what happens all too often, though. You will need about a weekend to replace a MacPherson strut tower, always assuming you have had some metalworking experience before. If you have never tackled a job like this, do not start on a MacPherson strut tower without experience. It is just a little bit too complicated for a complete novice, and you can really feel foolish if you make a hash of the job, and have to call in a professional! The cost of the material would be between £10 and £15 per side if you do the work yourself. That's not very much if it will extend the life of your car by another 20–30 years. Have a look at some of the photographs of the MacPherson strut tower in this book and decide if you think you could safely do the job. The correct way to go about it is like this:

1. Put some sort of protective blanket or dust cover over the engine. Then with a rotating wire brush get rid of all the loose rust, paint and underseal used to disguise the area.

2. When you have done this, have a good poke round with your trusty screwdriver. If there is just some ragged metal left, but the thicker top of the strut tower is still good, you can go ahead and patch. However, if the strut tower is badly corroded you are going to have to consider some major surgery.

   You will probably find that the vertical parts of the strut tower have not rusted much—perhaps only the top inch or so, where they are welded to the upper pan.

3. Once the suspension unit and all the other mechanicals

have been removed, get the hammer and chisel out and break the spot welds holding the verticals to the inner wing. Although we said that it is probably in good condition, it makes a much neater job to replace the whole assembly.

4. Break all the spot welds and remove the verticals. The job is much easier if the wing is removed. However, you can still do the job if the wings are left in place. On some cars it might be a simple job just to unbolt a wing.

5. The round pan which forms the top of the tower will probably be badly rusted. It is welded to the verticals, to the top of the inner wing and to the side of the inner wing. It will take a fair bit of effort to release all the spot welds. The discouraging part comes when you remove the top and find that there is very little metal left in the inner wing. In some cases you have to replace a section of the inner wing. Your repair will form two thicknesses

How not to do things. A great chunk of floor has been replaced with sheets of steel, while several important outriggers have vanished!

of metal. The first or lower thickness is the strut top, the second is the inner wing. You might also decide to plate the top with a proprietary repair patch. This will then mean three thicknesses of steel.

6. I like to assemble the tower top and verticals with clamps and bolts. The top can be bolted using the three bolts which hold the strut in place.

7. When all is assembled, and the parts fit well together, tack weld them in place.

8. The original line where the verticals were removed should still be visible. Now it is just a matter of welding the verticals into place, following the original line of spot welds.

9. You might need to dress the tower top so that its edge touches the inner wing. This is important to gain extra strength. Try to aim for about 1 to 2 in. of weld in this region. This is more than when the car was originally built, but will do no harm.

10. When all the welding is done, immediately treat the steel with rust inhibitor or primer. A good heavy undercoat completes the job underneath.

Anyone with some metalworking experience should be able to do a repair to one side in a weekend. Once again do not depend on having the car ready in a few hours. This is when jobs start to go wrong and get bodged. Take your time and it will last another 25 years.

As I have already mentioned, I would not recommend you try this as a first job. It can really put you off when you get to the point where all the old strut is off and you have the daunting prospect of welding the new one on. If the job is beyond you, there is no harm or shame in passing it to a professional. You can always try your hand at something a little easier.

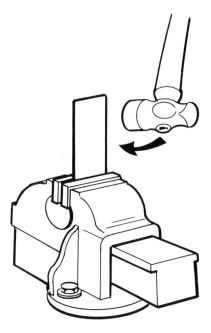

How to bend sheet metal in a vice. You could place a flat tyre lever between the hammer and the steel to prevent the steel being marked

Chapter 4 | Getting the old part off

In this chapter I want to have a look at getting the old rusty parts out, prior to welding in the new. There are really two stages to this, where you either rough-cut the part out, or secondly where you cut and trim neatly. The first type of job is one you might well tackle in a scrap yard.

Let's assume you have had a bit of luck. You have found an old car, the same as yours, in a breaker's yard. You can use lots of parts from it but how do you remove a piece of the chassis?

The short answer to this is by hard work. If you are lucky you can persuade the breaker to cut the bit off with his cutting torch. (By the way, I have found that very few breakers will allow you to bring your own cutting torch into their yard). If you cannot get it cut off, you will have to do it the hard way, with a hammer and a good sharp chisel.

But before you start hacking away, carefully examine the part. Get a sturdy screwdriver and start to poke, prod, scrape and generally examine the donor chassis. Don't be afraid of a bit of vandalism. If the chassis is rotten, prove it now, not when you cut it out and take it home.

Scrape off as much paint and underseal as you can from any areas which you think (or know, from your own car) are suspect. What you know about your own make and model will help you a great deal when you get into the breaker's yard. A little bit of know-how will save you hours and money. Every car rusts eventually. Some merely do it quicker than others.

You can save a fortune if you find the parts you want in a breaker's yard. For example, I once wanted a complete rear chassis section and a rear wing for a Volvo 144. When I heard the Volvo prices I nearly died. But I found what I

If you decide to build a London–Sydney Marathon replica Hillman Hunter, you will need some of these replacement parts. (Reproduced by permission of LMC Panels)

Hillman
Hunter/New Minx
1967 onwards

Sunbeam
Rapier/Alpine

Humber
Sceptre

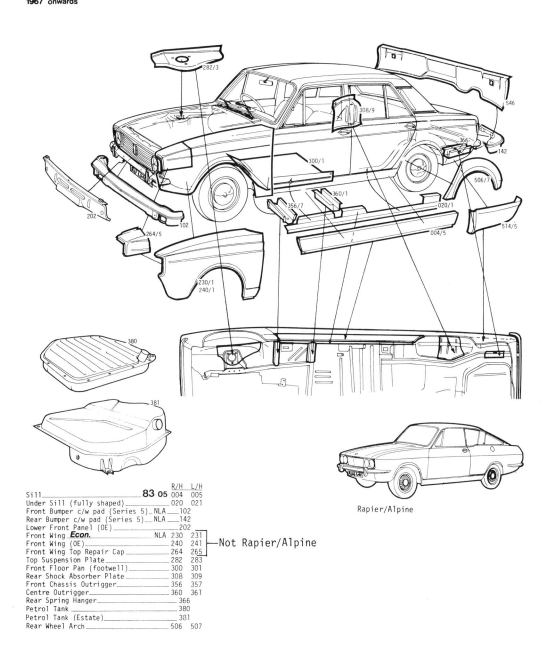

Rapier/Alpine

	R/H	L/H
Sill_____**83 05**	004	005
Under Sill (fully shaped)_____	020	021
Front Bumper c/w pad (Series 5)__NLA___	102	
Rear Bumper c/w pad (Series 5)__NLA___	142	
Lower Front Panel (OE)_____	202	
Front Wing *Econ.*_____NLA	230	231
Front Wing (OE)_____	240	241
Front Wing Top Repair Cap_____	264	265
Top Suspension Plate_____	282	283
Front Floor Pan (footwell)_____	300	301
Rear Shock Absorber Plate_____	308	309
Front Chassis Outrigger_____	356	357
Centre Outrigger_____	360	361
Rear Spring Hanger_____	366	
Petrol Tank _____	380	
Petrol Tank (Estate)_____	381	
Rear Wheel Arch_____	506	507

Not Rapier/Alpine

The author's Volvo pick-up
The entire rear quarter panel
and the associated chassis cost
just a full tank of petrol from a
scrapyard

wanted in a scrapyard and it was very cheap.

The breaker had half of a Volvo lying in the back of his yard. It had been stripped of all useful parts, so he thought of it as just scrap metal value. He agreed to cut off what I wanted and a few days later I picked it up with a trailer and took it home.

Normally, if you ask a scrapyard about buying chassis or monocoque parts they will look at you as though you were from another planet. They can understand anyone wanting a wing or a bonnet, but chassis parts—never!

When you locate the parts you want and agree the price, try to mark where you want the breaker to cut. You can either show him, or mark it with some sort of marker pen. Remember to allow about 6–12 in. more than you actually need. This allows for trimming and cleaning up.

If the yard will not cut it for you, then ask if you can hammer and chisel it out. This is not quite as daunting as it sounds. In the past I have had complete front ends off several cars. It usually costs you about an hour and a skinned knuckle.

Don't spend too much time being neat. Decide where you want to cut, allow some extra as we have said, and just hack away.

Once you have parted the bits you want from the car, you are faced with the problem of moving it. First you have to get it out of the yard, then home. A trailer is ideal for this but make sure you do not have any dangerous or jagged overhangs. (I would not advise you to press your luck and ask the yard to deliver. You might get an answer which was less than polite!)

When you get it home, again check to see which part you actually want. Again leave some extra. If you want a part which quite clearly joins another part, still leave yourself some extra. In other words don't cut at the join, cut beyond it. You will need that little bit of extra when you come to trim or grind.

Let me take the time now to explain how to remove spot welds. There are three distinct ways to remove or break a spot weld. The first method is to drill through the top layer of steel with a $\frac{1}{4}$ or $\frac{1}{16}$ in. drill. You do not need to drill

Don't be afraid of a little vandalism when removing parts from scrap cars. The person who removed this door pillar from a Volvo had the right idea. Take plenty of metal either side of the part you want

Not quite as tidy as it should be, but the wiring is well protected and the carpets are out of the way. The new outrigger is in place and a few hours will have it back on the road, good as new

through both surfaces unless you intend to 'puddle weld' the parts together again. (Puddle welding is described later).

The second way is with hammer and chisel. As spot welds occur every inch or so, force the chisel between the surfaces in between two welds. Cut through the welds with firm blows from the hammer. The sharper the chisel, the easier the job. Remember that this method can cause distortion if the steel is not supported. If your chisel is blunt, you will start to tear the spot weld rather than break it. This tear can either rip across the part you want or the scrap section. Keep the chisel sharp.

The third method uses a Sykes-Pickavant tool called a Zipcut Spot Weld Remover. This is fitted to an electric drill with a maximum speed of 900 rpm. A reversible cutting blade separates the two sheets of steel by drilling round the spot weld. The cutting head can be adjusted for various thicknesses of metal, so that only one thickness is actually cut. Spare blades are available. The tool is low priced.

Set to work with whichever method you have available and remove the 'scrap'. This takes time. You will probably notice that the bit you want is getting smaller, but the scrap pile is getting bigger. This is still acceptable. If you have marked out what you want, you cannot go wrong.

Once all the scrap is off, get the grinder out and clean up all the joining lips and flanges. Take off as much paint and underseal as possible. If you are going to weld the part into your car straight away, grind it down to bare metal to be sure of a sound welded join.

If you encounter a rusted nut, heat it with the welding torch until it starts to get red. Then put a socket on it. Gently put some pressure on the nut until it starts to turn. *Do not* try to bend the screw. When the nut starts to move, it will make a terrible screaming noise, but will still move. You may have to repeat the heat process before you get it off completely. *Do not* burn your fingers. *Always* replace a nut taken off this way.

Believe me, you get a really satisfying feeling when, after a couple of hours of effort, you have a nice, clean, sound, secondhand chassis member lying on your garage floor.

You might be unlucky at this point and find a little bit of rust which will need attention. But if you checked the part thoroughly before you removed it in the yard, you will have little to worry about. Remember this too, you did not have the part before. So even if it does need a little bit of attention, you are still ahead of the game!

Now that you have either bought or recovered a chassis part for your car, we will have a look at getting the old part off your vehicle.

If you know that you will be doing an extensive restoration job, it might be worthwhile having the underside of your vehicle sand blasted. This is usually only practical if you have a fully stripped bodyshell which can be turned over. It is possible to drive a car to the sandblaster, but you will find that the process leaves so much sand and dust that you will spend weeks trying to

Just one of the soft plastic bottles which you should have around at all times when the torch is lit. They prove an ideal back-up for a real fire extinguisher

Petrol tanks can be protected by coating them in fibreglass resin and mat. This one should last forever

clear it up. The sand works its way into all sorts of corners, and leaves quite a mess.

But if you are going to strip out the car anyway, it may not matter too much. The sand is blasted from a gun at high pressure and it will remove most things which get in its way. It can also damage rusty metal, so be very careful before handing over your car to this process. A better plan might be to have individual parts sandblasted. For example, a secondhand floor pan can quickly be cleaned up without too much trouble. If the operator is doing another job, you may be able to have your part blasted without too much expense.

Stripping a chassis or monocoque

It is difficult to give step by step instructions for a removal job, as I will have to explain the reasons for doing something a little later on, but this is a good guide:

1. Remove all carpets from the area to be worked on.
2. Remove all sound deadening panels, plastic sheets or underseal from the inside of the car.
3. Remove all other dirt, debris, plastic bags, or cigarette packets.
4. If any wiring is exposed by removing the carpets, make sure it is moved safely out of the way.
5. Jack up the side of the car you want to work on. Support the car with axle stands or ramps. Do *not* use bricks.
6. Take the new part and match it to the underside of the car or the chassis. Have you got the correct part? Is it a sided part? Have you got the correct side?

The front jacking point looks all right from here, but the centre crossmember will fail, being corroded where it meets the inner sill. This is a very common repair job

These captive nuts are normally used to secure front wings. They can be used for other things and it is useful to have half a dozen handy when working on a car

7. If removing a top hat section, decide if it will weaken the structure of the bodyshell. If it will you will have to support the rest of the shell with wood or in extreme cases provide extra stiffening. Normally you would not be tackling such a big job as this in one go.

8. To remove rusty steel, I prefer to use a hammer and chisel. WEAR GOGGLES! A cutting torch puts too much heat into the part and this spreads to surrounding areas. You can cut with a welding nozzle, all you have to do is to turn the oxygen level up. If you have an angle grinder you can cut away most of the outrigger, but you will still have to resort to hammer and chisel in the end.

9. When most of the scrap part is gone, you are left with the $\frac{1}{4}$ in. lips, spot welded to the floor of the car. I use an old $\frac{1}{4}$ in. screwdriver to deal with this. After you get most of it off, use a grinder or chisel to clean the job up. This job takes a lot of time, and is dirty and unpleasant. However, the neater the job of removal, the neater the final, finished repair is going to be.

10. When all of the old part is off, once again offer up the new part to see if you have a tight fit, a loose fit, or no fit at all. If you have a tight fit you can dress the $\frac{1}{4}$ in. lips back to provide a bit more clearance. If too slack, you can dress the lips forward to make them a closer fit to the main parts of the chassis. If necessary make small cuts in the lips to allow adjustment.

11. When you have achieved a nice firm fit, the next problem is how to keep the part in place prior to welding.

The best way is to use a screw jack and a block of wood. The outrigger can be man-handled into place. Then with a bit of practice the jack is screwed up to press the outrigger into place. If you are lucky enough to have the car really high then you will have to put a block of wood between the jack and the chassis. Do not exert too much pressure on the jack or you will start to lift the car. This can cause damage as an area without the strength of the fully fitted chassis is much weaker.

I often use a bolt inserted into the captive nuts in a floor section to locate little pieces of heavy gauge scrap steel and washers which can be encouraged to pull the

outrigger tightly against the floor section. You will get wise to these little tricks as you go along.

Once you decide to start welding you have to think about safety all the time.

Jaguars rust! Just in front of the door pillar, above the sill is some dreaded corrosion which will need a little welding

Safety

Before lighting the torch to weld a panel on a car, there are a number of jobs which need to be done to ensure safety and a satisfactory repair. Welding involves high temperatures, so the first safety check is to consider any item in the car surrounding the working area which might catch fire. Have another look at the last list of instructions. We will run through them again in some more detail.

If a new floor pan is being installed, then all round the area should be carefully examined for paint, underseal, underfelt, carpets, electrical wiring, old cigarette packets—in fact anything which might burn.

Paint can be removed with a wire brush in an electric

drill, and it should be removed at least an extra inch round the area to be welded. Underneath the panel there may be paint or underseal or bitumen. The latter can burn fiercely and if it drips onto the skin it can cause a very painful burn.

Scrape away all underseal from the surrounding area; it only takes a few minutes with the wire brush, while a burn takes weeks to heal properly.

Underfelt can often prove troublesome, as it sometimes seems to be bonded to the body with the gripping power of an octopus. Again a rotating wire brush can often help, but scrape away as much as you can with a hand-held brush, and save the more expensive rotating brush from getting hopelessly tangled.

Removing the carpets seems so obvious, but it is often overlooked. If at all possible, the entire carpet should be removed, but if not, lift as much of the carpet as you can. They are often in two or three pieces and connected with press-studs. If you cannot lift the carpet for any reason, ensure that it is pulled back as far from the welding area as possible. Here are a few tips for securing carpets: A number of spring-type clothes pegs will hold a carpet against a convenient door or steering wheel. A few pieces of string tied round carpet corners and tied to a nearby point such as a door handle will do just as well. Finally, for heavier or more stubborn carpets a few crocodile clips (like the ones used on the ends of jump leads) will prove ideal.

Wiring looms are often a nuisance when you are welding. Sometimes they can be overlooked due to the dirt or they do not look close enough to the welding area to cause any problem.

Have a good look at any wiring runs near the proposed welding area, and if there is any possibility of damaging a loom by heat, use either the clothes peg method or crocodile clips to pull the loom clear. There is little point in burning a perfectly good wiring loom for the sake of a few minutes' work.

Some of these points are so obvious, but when you are keen to get on with the job, they *can* be overlooked with disastrous results.

You might find it necessary to remove a seat to gain extra room to weld part of the floor. Normally seats are held to

Above left **MG Midget it says on the sill, and there is only a small amount of rust but it will still require attention. Mud builds up on this ledge**

Below left **Here most of the sill has been removed. The remaining ridge is the part spot welded to the inner sill. It can be chiselled off. I used a big screwdriver to open up the flanges between spot welds to allow the chisel in**

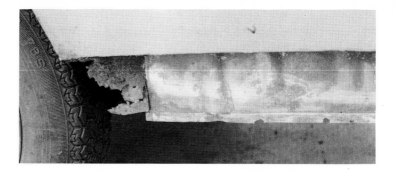

Top **The old sill has been chiselled off leaving just the remains of the blanking piece. Now is the time to take a cardboard pattern for this part**

Above **This odd view shows a Triumph Herald's backbone cut through. The outrigger shows typical rust damage. You can also see where the body is secured to the chassis**

their mountings by four bolts and it is sometimes difficult to find these bolts without moving both the carpet and the underfelt. If you take the seat out, it gives you an opportunity to give it a good clean.

A word of warning with plastic upholstery: Do not take *any* chances! Apart from the difficulty of matching a damaged seat, if the material catches fire poisonous fumes are given off; these fumes can cause sickness, and in severe cases unconciousness and death. If you are in any doubt, remove the upholstery. Time taken now will be saved later. A blazing seat will, in less time than it takes to read this sentence, spread the fire to the headlining and door panels. Your car is then a write-off. I know someone who wishes he had paid more attention to this point after he set fire to his recently re-built and re-sprayed Cortina 1600E. He tried to pull the burning seats out but was beaten by the noxious fumes.

Don't take any chances!

Having taken all possible precautions, here are a few more hints for home welders. As well as your fire extinguisher, keep half a dozen plastic 'Squeezy' bottles handy, filled with water. One of them can be kept with the welding equipment. They hold a useful amount of water and they will not spill if accidentally knocked over. They cost nothing and when squeezed will push out quite a powerful stream of water which can be used in an emergency. Do not think they will replace fire extinguishers, though.

And lastly, another emergency aid for putting out a small fire is a can of beer. Keep one handy and if you have to use it, give it a good shake to get it nice and lively, before pulling the ring and letting it spray over the fire. This tip came from a fireman, and you should keep it in mind. Pity about the beer, though!

NEVER allow splashes of hot metal to reach your skin, especially when welding underneath the car. WEAR GLOVES. I used to be careless about this until a small lump of red-hot metal got inside my watch-strap and taught me a painful lesson.

NEVER support a car with bricks. They have been known to explode under a heavy weight, and you do not want to be underneath when they do.

Petrol tanks

The repair of petrol tanks is to be covered in the 'Carburation' book in this series. However, since we might be working near a tank it is best if you know how to treat them safely.

It is best if the tank is completely removed, but if you decide not to remove it, then be sure to drain out all the petrol. Blow compressed air into the tank to remove all the fumes and dry up any remaining dregs of fuel. Alternatively, run a pipe from a car exhaust into the tank and let the exhaust gases purge the tank. Adequate ventilation must be available if you choose this method.

Finally, having done the above, if you intend to weld

Typical inner sill damage. The new outrigger needs some new inner sill to weld to! You can see the rust line which provides a guide for cutting out rot

close to the tank, fill it completely with water. When I say completely, I mean just that. Also rock the tank to make sure there are no pockets of trapped vapour. Fill the tank up to the overflowing point.

When you finish welding, you will need to repeat the compressed air or exhaust gas purge to dry up the water. At this point it is also worth sloshing some petrol round the tank to pick up any remaining moisture. This petrol must then be disposed of safely.

Remember to blow through all the petrol pipes you disconnected when a tank is removed. Petrol can back syphon from a bowl and the last thing you want is to have petrol dripping out when you are welding.

(Did you know that you can coat the outside of a petrol tank with fibreglass mat and resin? This will ensure that it never rusts).

NEVER weld without a fire extinguisher handy.

Chapter 5 | **Fitting a new part**

For normal chassis welding you need an oxy-acetylene outfit like the Portapac kit described later, in chapter seven. Normally, you will expect to use a Number 2 tip in the BOC Sapphire torch. Other equipment will have other sizes, so contact the supplier and ask their advice.

Chassis members are normally constructed from 16 or 18 gauge steel, while floor pans and other panels are made from 20 gauge. BOC recommend a Number 1 tip for floor-pan thickness and a Number 2 for chassis leg thickness.

Most monocoque chassis welding is done above your head, unless you are lucky enough to have one of those devices which allows a car to be turned on to its side. Lying it on its side will make welding ten times easier for you, but if there is then any problem which requires access to the inside of the car, such as burning sealer, it makes for a very dangerous situation, trying to open a door on top of the car.

Most of us will have to do our chassis restorations lying on the ground. This makes it a fair-weather sport! The biggest problem then is getting the car high enough to be useful.

I have just measured the distance from the tip of my welding torch to my elbow. It is about 30 in. Ideally, you need to lift the car by 30 in. What happens in practice is that you might be able to jack up and use axle stands, gaining some 18–20 in. if you are lucky. To compensate for this restricted room, you alter the angle of the torch and lose the magic 60 degrees which is the ideal angle the torch should make with the steel.

Next, you end up trying to gain a better position by moving about relative to the seam to be welded. Perhaps you have good access to one chassis side, but not the other.

I cannot give you any magic answers. I began my welding career using a water-filled pit (complete with frog), but this gave me problems when I wanted to get to the inside of the car.

The best suggestion I can make, apart from buying a set of very high ramps, is to jack up the vehicle on which you are working, as high as possible, and then do a little bit of welding at a time. It is extremely hard on the neck muscles and on the arm holding the torch and I have often resorted to leaning my head against a spare wheel to gain some support.

This is one of the reasons why I say, never make a firm estimate. The job always takes longer than you think, for all the reasons which you have forgotten. Jacking up and making safe takes time, and when your neck starts to protest you get fed up pretty quickly. This is the time when the job will be spoilt.

Remember that what you are doing can be expected to last some 20–30 years if it is protected properly. So do it just once—and do it right. Don't bodge, don't skimp and don't do only half a job. If the car has to be off the road while the work is being done, make alternative arrangements.

Most work is done in small lockup garages, or in the open air. Do not forget safety, and when you have finished welding for the day, remember to visit the car again about half an hour later to check that you have left nothing smouldering.

This method proved very effective in keeping the door open during work on the sills. The wings are next!

Get some paint or primer onto the welds as soon as possible, otherwise the rust process will start up again as soon as you shut off the torch.

Let's have a look at some individual items which might cause you problems. For vertical welding, start at the bottom and work up. Move the torch and filler rod in a semi circle. When you start to use a new rod, fold the last inch over so that you have a little hook. This is for two reasons:

1. It tells you which is the hot end, and
2. It also prevents you sticking the rod in your eye. (You *must* wear goggles all the time you are welding, but accidents can still happen when you shut off the torch).

If you are welding into a tight corner and the flame keeps blowing out, try drilling a hole in the corner to reduce the pressure build-up.

Occasionally, you will need to replace a captive nut—one which is welded or brazed onto the bodyshell to locate some other component.

Select the correct nut. Make sure its threads are in good shape by running a bolt through it. Drill the necessary hole in a piece of steel, or in the chassis. Make sure the bolt passes through the hole.

The old favourite, the Morris Minor. Although this one has had some nice neat welding done to the rear spring hanger, the car has retired to the breaker's yard

Place the nut on the plate and hold it in place by tightening the bolt. Braze the nut into place. Release the bolt while it is still hot.

Now for a look at some other areas which will need welding.

Jacking points
Jacking points can be classified in several categories; the kind where a steel tube lies parallel to the road and the second kind, where a hole is drilled in a reinforced part of the chassis and a jack locates from underneath. The third kind is just a reinforced flat plate. The jack is put underneath and lifts directly onto the reinforcing.

The steel tube type are best replaced rather than repaired. If possible track down a replacement part. If this fails, try to adapt one from another car from the same manufacturer. If all else fails, buy a suitable piece of steel pipe from a steel supplier and copy the existing jacking point.

The other side of the same Morris Minor. It seems a pity that this car has been scrapped after such efforts to restore it

The reinforced type can be repaired more easily, but the heavier gauge of steel used means you will have to use a larger nozzle in the torch. The flat plate type require similar treatment.

I have already told you how I adapted a rear leg as a front outrigger on a Mk I Cortina. On another Ford, this time a Classic/Capri, I have used an MGB jacking point welded to a front box section as I could not find an original part. While researching this book, I have just noticed the Cortina Mk II front jacking point. It looks as though it might be rather useful on other cars. Remember those catalogues and parts books. This is when they come in handy!

Spare wheel wells

There are basically two kinds of spare wheel wells. One type holds the wheel vertically and consists of a semi-circle built into the floor. Normally it is built at one side of the boot, so the wheel stands against the rear wing panel, or the side of the compartment.

The second type consists of a flat well in the boot floor. The spare wheel lies down in this well which is usually covered by a hardboard sheet and some carpet.

The vertical type suffers from rust due to water collecting in the bottom of the well. There is usually a rubber grommet with a hole in it, to let water out, but it clogs up fairly quickly. This type of well can be repaired in sections which are butt welded into position. Make sure you drill an adequate drain hole, and protect the new steel with extra rust inhibitor and underseal.

The flat well rusts for the same reasons, although it always looks worse because of the large flat area involved. Again, you can make up repair panels which are butt welded into position. You might be lucky and get a reasonably sound wheel well from a scrap car, or one which has suffered front-end accident damage.

Crossmembers

Big crossmembers such as engine crossmembers and gearbox supports do not really concern us too much. They rarely rust, as they are built of very heavy steel. All they

British Oxygen's very popular Portapak gas welding set. You can buy these from BOC or quite often rent them from the many hire shops throughout the country

need is a rub down and fresh paint.

Any rubber mounting bushes should be replaced, as they can deteriorate over the years, especially if they have been soaked in oil.

Crossmembers are normally bolted to the floor using captive nuts. If something goes wrong here, such as a broken bolt, or captive nut which has come loose, you will have to open up the chassis member to get at the fault. A Monodex cutter is good for this, as it just needs a pilot hole drilled to get it started. Remember that three sides of a box section are heavy gauge, while the fourth side is lighter. Open up the fourth, or lighter, side.

The other types of crossmembers are the pressed steel variety which sometimes make up the front and rear of the chassis. The rear one often supports the petrol tank. Let's look at the rear crossmember first.

Often they are not true box sections—being a pressing

This breaker's yard photograph shows the corrosion which attacks the spare wheel well. It is quite a simple job to replace these rusty parts with home-made repair panels

from a flat sheet of steel. Their strength comes from the shape built into them. They have curves and strengthening grooves stamped in at the factory. Remember, that you can make bends by hammering (this is described in chapter 6) but the best plan is to try to obtain a new or good secondhand crossmember, as it could be difficult to make a new one due to the complex shape. Make a paper, then a cardboard template. Often you will have to make the templates in two halves, due to the size of the crossmember. If possible simplify the shape, so that you can reproduce it more easily.

Remember, you will probably have to remove the petrol tank to repair the crossmember. Don't take short cuts!

The rear crossmember may run very close to the rear valance, so you will have to take into account its relationship with all these parts.

A simple starting point for a crossmember replacement

This Ford 100E battery box has seen better times. It forms part of the inner wing and would make a nice repair job. However, the condition of the rest of the car was just as bad, so it was scrapped

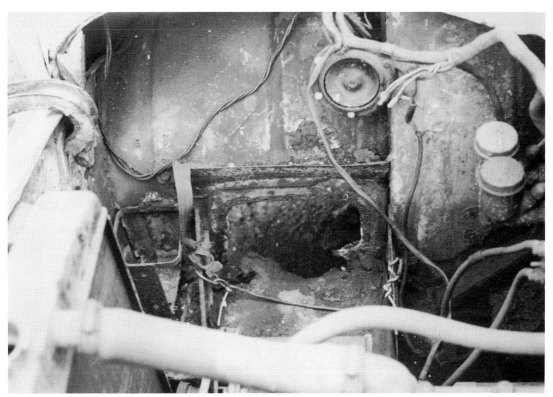

This is the type of jacking point which is basically a steel tube parallel to the road. Look through the body spares catalogues to match it, if you cannot get the real thing

would be a strip of steel with a 90-degree fold at each end and another 90-degree fold running along both the top and the bottom. The top one is to weld into the chassis, the lower for strength. You can add strengthening grooves by hammering. See the photographs with the shoemakers' last.

Check any holes which have to be drilled; also ascertain any captive nuts which have to be fixed on, perhaps for an exhaust pipe mounting bracket. You may also have to drill a hole for wiring, such as for a reversing light, or petrol tank sender unit. Protect wiring with a rubber grommet.

Front crossmembers are different, often consisting of a box section, so a repair may be slightly easier than a replacement. You may only have to weld one side of the box. The radiator and possibly some suspension parts may have to be removed to allow this type of repair. If you do open up a box section, remember to clean out all the dirt and debris. If the original had drain holes, you will have to allow for these in your repair. Larger holes can be made with a chassis punch as described in chapter two. You can make large slots by overlapping several of these chassis punch holes, then filing the profile smooth.

Remember to leave the $\frac{1}{4}$ in. lips at either side to weld to the main chassis members.

You can make all these parts, given time. The annoying thing is that if you then make the part a second time it invariably comes out ten times better. The problem is always time. Take your time, and do the job slowly and methodically. Don't create metalwork which leaves you embarrassed to open the bonnet!

Battery boxes

Battery boxes corrode due to rust from the underneath and spilt acid from above. This is much rarer with the new generation of sealed batteries, but older cars may have suffered in the past. The tray often collects dirt and moisture which is held by a rubber mat on which the battery sits.

First, try to find a replacement battery box from the breaker's yard. If you cannot you will have to repair your own. Mini owners are lucky, they can buy a new box which just welds into place. (Can you adapt one of these for your car?)

Fords have a platform on which the battery sits. It is held in place by supporting wire straps. Most repairs can be completed by making up a new floor section, having taken a template from the original. Just add some extra drain holes, and treat the steel with rust inhibitor when it is welded in place.

Rubber bushes

Rubber bushes are used to mount mechanical parts such as springs, to the chassis. If you have to replace a rear chassis leg, the rear spring hanger will have to be released. Look at the workshop manual for your particular car. You will probably have to support the rear axle while the rear hanger is released. Try to obtain new rubber bushes before

This is a made up repair part for a jacking point. The steel tube will fit in the groove. It will be fitted the other way up

This MGB jacking point has already found a use in my 1963 Ford Capri. It makes an ideal jacking point replacement for many cars. It's cheap too! . .

you start this job. It is no good re-fitting old, worn, or cracked and decayed rubber bushes.

Rubber bushes will harden if exposed to the welding torch. After that they will ignite and burn with a choking black smoke. Molten rubber often drips off. Don't take any chances. If they are to be refitted, remove the bushes and store them in a safe place.

Spring mountings

Rust in a spring mounting, especially the front mounting, is a serious problem. Some cars, for example the Morris Minor, have new spring hangers available for welding in. This makes the job easier. Refer to your catalogues and lists if you need a spring hanger for your car. If you cannot get a new one, have a look for a secondhand one from a scrap vehicle.

If you cannot locate one, you will have to make one. Look at the workshop manual for instructions on how to remove the spring.

You might find it easier to make up the spring mounting on the car. Find out the thickness of the original steel by using a wire gauge or micrometer. The correct location is vital, as you must not weld in a spring mounting $\frac{1}{8}$ in. out of place. The hammer and chisel will help you to dismantle the mounting. Dismantle one side or piece at a time, then make a template for the new part. Next, make the new steel part and try it against the remaining parts of the mounting. In this way you get the closest possible replica of the original.

Do not skimp either time or materials on this sort of repair. If you are worried about tackling it, refer it to a professional. Do it properly, because it is a very important part of a chassis.

Hot shrinking

If you find that a floor panel is a bit too flexible after you have fitted it, do not despair. There is a technique known as shrinking which can help. Actually there are two kinds of shrinking, hot shrinking and cold shrinking. We will look at hot shrinking first.

In the good old days it was recommended that you

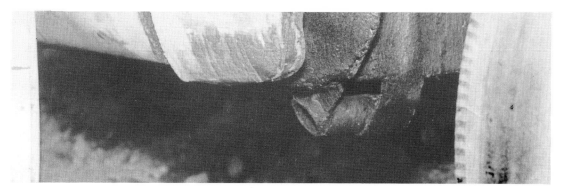

Above . . . and this is it, fitted.
The grooved steel on the
crossmember is a piece of steel
made 'grooved' in my last

Below **This Morris Minor inner
wing is pretty ragged. It could
be repaired or patched, but you
might be able to find a better
one on a scrap car**

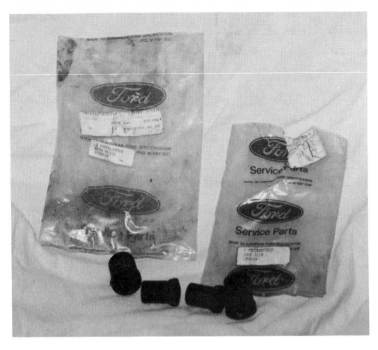

Don't spoil the job for the sake of a few rubber bushes. These are rear spring hanger bushes from Ford

needed a welding torch and a heap of wet asbestos. Nowadays even to use the word asbestos causes near panic. So I suppose the next best thing is to use a lot of shredded newspaper soaked in a bucket of water. What you want is a big soggy lump like porridge. As an alternative I suppose you could also use a bundle of wet rags.

Cover the bulging area (the area which flexes the most) with the soggy paper. Press the pulp down firmly onto the steel. Now poke your finger through the pulp, to the steel, to make a series of holes.

Light the welding torch and direct it into one of the holes near the outside of the pulp. Heat the steel to cherry red. Take the torch away and push the wet pulp into the hole. The hot metal will be quickly chilled. Repeat the process for the other holes, always working in towards the centre of the pulp. Four or five applications of torch then pulp should do the trick. Don't overdo it, and keep the pulp really wet.

There is an alternative to this method which needs a mallet or a proper shrinking hammer. You heat the centre of the stretched area, again to cherry red, then support the underneath of the hot spot with a flat dolly. Strike the hot area with a flat mallet or a shrinking hammer if one is available. This process brings about the same end result, and is favoured by many restorers.

That was hot shrinking. Cold shrinking is in some ways easier to accomplish.

What you need is a special dolly with a groove down it, or you can use a piece of large diameter tubing (say 1½ in.) Hold the dolly or tube under the flexing area, and strike the upper surface of the steel with the round, ball end of a hammer. Do not strike too hard, and keep checking the panel. What will happen is that the steel being hit, because it is not supported by the groove in the dolly, will be pushed down. This process takes the excess steel down into the hole and pulls the rest of the panel tighter. Once again, do not overdo the process and constantly check the result of your hammering. The same technique is used to put grooves in sheet steel to strengthen it.

You can use the same process to sink welds below the surface of the panel so that they can be hidden with filler or lead.

Always bend over the last few inches of a welding rod. It tells you that the other end might be hot, and stops you poking your eye out as well

Chapter 6 | **Patching**

The large, flat repair panel such as is fitted to the top of a MacPherson strut is one of the most common patching applications. If you cannot obtain a new repair patch from a dealer, you will have to make your own. Yet again, use paper to make the shape, followed by cardboard. Once you have got the correct shape cut out on card, use the card to mark out the steel plate.

You will need to cut a large hole to accommodate the top bearing of the MacPherson strut. To do this, lay the patch over the hole, in the correct position and run a pencil round the existing hole, so marking the diameter onto your new steel patch.

Mark the locations of the three mounting holes for the suspension unit. Drill these three holes next.

Now bolt the patch into place and check your markings for the large diameter hole. When this is finalized, drill a small hole just inside the marked circle. Then, with a Monodex type cutting tool, cut out a circular hole, following the line. You can then file the edges when the cut is finished. Carry out any rust treatment which is needed for the area under the patch. Having made a final check that everything is correct, bolt the patch in place and tack weld it. Dress the edges and complete the welding. When the welding is finished, smooth the welds with a grinder, and paint. It is possible to make an almost invisible repair if enough care is taken. Once again, do not rush the job.

Some general rules for patching; whether it is for strut tops or chassis repairs. Keep the area of overlap as small as possible. It is pointless covering rusty steel with new steel, as the rust will only lick its lips and start to spread to the new panel. A small area of the old panel is useful as a support for the new panel, but generally $\frac{1}{2}$ in. is the maximum overlap you should allow.

There are times when it is best to cut out a larger area than is strictly necessary. This would be done where the shape of the panel would help to hide the repair. Perhaps a ridge or bend determines a good cutting line. It is often easier to disguise a repair by welding along a seam or other noticeable feature.

Having said that, it is just as true to make a very small repair, say less than an inch square. Why put a large patch into an otherwise sound panel, if just one little hole is rusty. If you decide to use a small patch you will find it difficult to locate it prior to welding. Try these two tips:

Weld the end of a thin welding rod to the centre of the mini patch. The patch, which should be cut just slightly smaller than the hole, can now be held in place with one hand while a tack weld is completed.

Alternatively cut out the mini patch but leave two little lips or projections which will sit on the main panel. Weld the patch in position, then fuse in the extra lips, or grind them away.

Fabricating

Occasionally, you will need to make up a repair section

Below left **Two clamps and a steel strip are very useful when you want to bend a lip on a piece of sheet steel. You can tap the lip over with a hammer, or a flat tyre lever**

Below **This is the result of a few minutes hammering on the last. A groove is formed in the steel. This makes it much stronger than the un-grooved part**

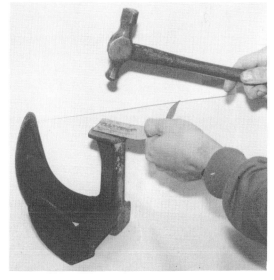

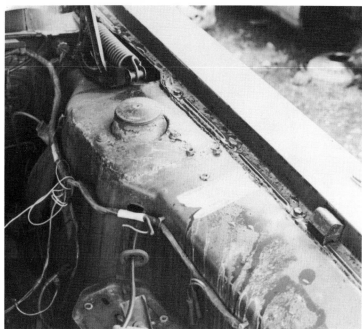

Above **Putting the groove in! It only takes a few minutes to make a part like this, using the round end of a staple hammer**

Above right **You can see where this MacPherson strut top has been welded. Although the welding looks fairly good, the rust is already making another attack on the new steel**

from several pieces of steel. If the shape is complex, and cannot be folded in a machine, then cut out a paper template for each part of the repair panel. Measure up and when the paper shape is correct, transfer to card, then steel.

Cut out the steel pieces and try them against the original. Next, tack weld the pieces together in the required shape, and offer them up to the chassis. If the shape is correct, complete the welding operation off the vehicle. Remember to weld only clean shiny steel. Do not try to weld over paint. Don't concentrate too much heat on any one area, otherwise distortion will result.

If you decide that you have to apply a patch to a section of top hat, there are some very old established guidelines available for this type of job. This is because similar patches were applied to prewar cars to repair great thick chassis sections.

The patch must not be cut out as a rectangle. Instead the top edge of the patch should be shorter than the bottom. The recommended angle between the bottom edge and the side edge is 60 degrees. Only the top and bottom edges of

the patch should be welded, otherwise a stress is built into the area and cracks could later result.

The height of the patch can also be adjusted to allow for a run of weld at top and bottom.

This MacPherson strut repair looks very neat, but the owner has still to finish the job by attaching the repair panel to the wing

Miscellaneous patching know-how

If you patch an area which might be seen, or if you are very particular and want to disguise a line of weld then you can 'sink' it. This is done with a hammer (the one you use to dress welds) and a special dolly known as a shrinking dolly. This type of dolly is illustrated in the book. It consists of a block of steel with a groove cut in one face. If the groove is placed below the steel, with the weld in the middle of the groove and parallel to it, the weld can be hammered down below the level of the panels. The depth to sink is about $\frac{3}{16}$ in. The groove formed can be filled with lead or plastic filler depending on your skill.

Small to medium sized patches should be dished if possible, so that their centres are at a slightly lower level than the edges. This is because the welding process, even if

Above **If a strut repair panel is not available for your car, make your own. This illustration will give you an idea of what to look for when marking out a cardboard shape. The hole is for the top bearing of the shock-absorber, while the cut-out is for the bonnet hinge**

Above right **Compare this with some of the other repair jobs. A home-made plate has been welded underneath the strengthening ring. The welding has been neatly finished with a grinder and has been primered and painted. That was over two years ago!**

carried out to avoid distortion, will cause the patch to 'rise' and expand. The result will be a patch which is much neater, and does not bulge.

Repairing a crack in a chassis section is not too difficult. However, try to establish the cause of the crack to avoid it happening again. I remember some Fords used to crack sometimes, behind the steering box. In fact one of my first Cortinas failed an MOT test for this reason.

The crack will often start from a bolt hole or some other fitment. Clean off the entire area so that you can see the extent of the damage. Next, drill a small (say, $\frac{1}{8}$ in. diameter) hole at the end of the crack. This will stop it spreading any further. When you are sure of the extent of the crack, weld the hole and the crack. Some authorities recommend brazing for this, but I cannot see any reason not to weld. Finish off the job by grinding, or filing, the weld to tidy it up. Then rustproof the area, prime it, and paint it.

Subframes

Mention subframes and everyone immediately thinks of

Minis and 1100s. Then they think of rust! Of course subframes rust, just like everything else, if not treated properly. But subframes have been used on many other cars.

Mini and 1100 subframes for instance, can be patched and a number of patch panels are available from the specialist manufacturers. If you are in any doubt about the condition of a subframe, I would recommend that you remove it from the car before making a final judgement. There is little enough room under a car, particularly a Mini, so do make things easier for yourself, and remove the subframe first.

If you buy a replacement, remember to treat the new or secondhand subframe with a rust inhibitor and plenty of primer and underseal.

If you are going to patch your existing subframe, follow the same rules as you would for any other patching job. Clean the steel, cut out the rust, weld in the new, and protect.

The point at which the subframe meets the body can often cause problems, but various parts are available from suppliers to overcome this problem. Once again, a look through some catalogues could save you a lot of time and trouble.

Curved patches
So far, we have only looked at straight line repair panels. But what happens if you need a curve? If you cannot buy the part needed, you would be stuck again. For example, you might want to weld in a patch between the wheelarch and the floor. For this you need a piece of steel bent at 90 degrees. One side is welded to the floor, the other to the wheelarch. But the wheelarch is curved. What can you do? The simple, time-honoured way is to cut some 'Vs' in the side to be welded to the floor. This allows the other side to be bent to the required shape.

However, there is another way. Spread the metal with a hammer, as described below, for the compound curve. If you want to bend the vertical side, hammer the horizontal side, and vice versa. This will give you a nice smooth curve. Try it on a piece of scrap and learn the principle in just a few minutes.

Above **A more advanced case of terminal rot. The repair panel here has been welded nicely, but the rust is now well advanced and the car is resting in the breaker's yard**

Above right **This MacPherson strut assembly could be cut out of this scrap car to provide a cheap replacement for a rust damaged one. Half an hour with hammer and chisel would do it!**

Once you have tried it this way, you will find it makes a neater job than using 'Vs'. The nice smooth curve is the one to use.

Compound curves

It is also quite easy to make a compound curve if you can weld. If you hammer a piece of steel it will expand and get thinner. The most common example given to illustrate this process is a piece of pastry. If you roll the pastry it will get bigger in area, but thinner in section. There is only a given quantity of pastry and it has to go somewhere.

You can do exactly the same with steel. Rolling can be done with expensive equipment, (see Bob Smith's *Sheet Metal Bodywork* book in this series) but for our purposes we are going to hammer. Try the following experiment:

Take a small piece of scrap steel about three or four

inches square. Fold a 90-degree lip of about $\frac{1}{4}$ in. Now, with your small staple hammer (or panel beating hammer) repeatedly strike the area of the $\frac{1}{4}$ in. lip. After a time, depending on how hard and how frequent your blows are, the lip will expand and get thinner, but the larger area of the steel will start to bend. If you kept on hammering you could almost make a semi-circle. Once again this is difficult to put into words, but have a look at the photographs, then try it. It only takes a few minutes to learn.

Now having proved to you that you can do it, the next step is to appreciate that you have made a curve in one direction only. What you want is a piece of steel with a shape like the curves on a football. From any point on the surface, each curve moves in many directions, to give you a ball-shape. The rear valance has a compound curve at each end. It is difficult to make this shape unless you make it in two (or even three) pieces.

This repair has been made where the rear wheelarch meets the boot floor—a favourite place for the rust bug

Above **Another view of that wheelarch repair. The dark part of the boot floor came from answering an advert in the owners club magazine!**

Right **You can have 'top hat' sections made up by the local sheet metal shop. These two chassis legs were made from one three-foot length and cost just a few pounds. The end pieces were gas welded**

Cut the required piece of steel. Make a right-angled turn of about $\frac{1}{4}$ in. Start to hammer the lip with your panel hammer, or the pein face if you have this type of hammer. As the metal stretches, a curve will form. Keep on checking the shape of the curve against the original or pattern. (Once again, let me remind you—*never* throw away any body parts, no matter how rusty, until you have completed the repair, or replaced the part with a new one). Keep on checking until you have got the curve right.

Once you have got the first part of the curve right, make up another paper template for the next part of the curve. You will have to make a part like a corner piece out of two or three separate pieces which you have to weld together. Have a look at the photographs which will make everything clear.

This technique is useful in that it teaches you to line up two or more parts accurately and encourages your welding techniques. The finished article will be in a prominent place, being an outer panel.

Wheelarches
Wheelarch repairs present similar problems, the main difference being that you have to form a simple curve in the steel. To do this, use any sort of round former which will help you create the shape; telephone poles, dustbins, or beer barrels all have useful shapes. Don't forget that an old wheel and tyre might have a very similar shape to the required wheelarch! Try to get the shape as near correct as possible, as it will result in a neat job. Once again, only weld clean steel, and do not risk distortion by welding too long in one area.

Grooving
If you take a large sheet of steel, it will flex in the middle under its own weight. You can build in extra strength by hammering or forming grooves in the steel. This prevents flexing, and also stiffens up the steel panel.

To make your own grooves, either you need a shrinking dolly, or a small piece of steel pipe, of about 1 in. in diameter. Place the dolly or the open end of the tube under the steel where you want the groove. Hammer the steel

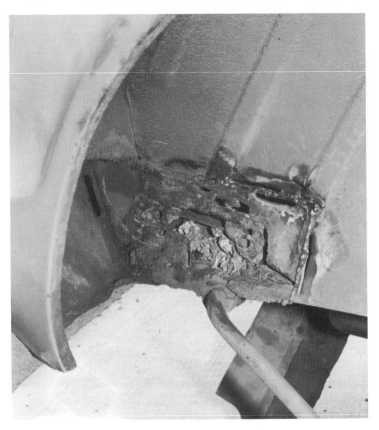

Above **This is what I found inside the chassis leg. There is paint, anti-rust treatment and silver paper. I have no idea how it got in there, as there has been no work done on this car before!**

Right **The old steel has been cut away with hammer and chisel and some cleaning up has been done to the inside of the box section. It was in fairly good condition after 22 years**

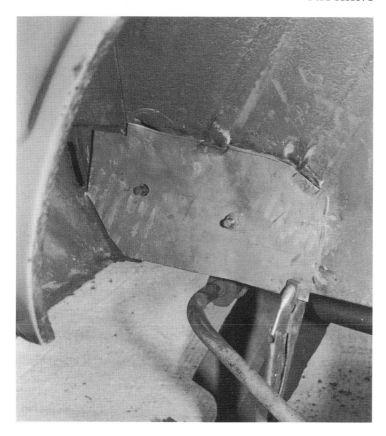

with a round pein face of a hammer. The steel will be stretched and pushed down into the unsupported area. Move the dolly or tube along the line you want the groove to take. Do not strike the steel too hard. A slow controlled stretch is what you want. Again, I refer you to the photographs.

I use a shoemaker's last with a groove for grooving small pieces of steel. It works as if designed for the job!

The new patch is held in place by the bumper bolts and a pair of Mole grips. Where the inner wing is ribbed, I have made suitable cuts in the steel plate. Everything in place and ready for the torch. This patch should last another 22 years at least

Seat belt mountings

If you are restoring a car built before 1965 you might decide to fit seat belts. (Cars registered in the UK before January 1965 do not need seat belts to be fitted, but if they *are*, they must be worn by the driver and front seat passenger).

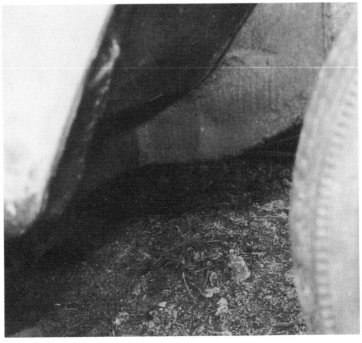

Above **Not the neatest of patches, but this little Honda Civic has lived to fight many another day. The repair is a mixture of pop rivets and weld and is heavily disguised with underseal**

Right **A common place for Fords to rust. This owner has made a good attempt at repairing the inner front wheelarch. The repair is sound, and is well protected with paint and underseal**

Belt mountings will have to be fitted to the floor and a general requirement is that the mounting should pass through a piece of steel about $\frac{1}{4}$ in. thick and about 4 sq. in. in area.

This spare wheel well is being repaired in three sections. The first two sections have been welded in, and the third section is just about to be fitted

This plate is fitted on the outside of the car and can be welded in position if required. Plates are often supplied by the seat belt manufacturer, but if you have to make your own do not use anything thinner than $\frac{1}{4}$ in. or smaller than 4 sq. in.

When welding the plate in position, do not damage the seat belt with heat. Remember to work safely. Similarly, if you are fitting non-standard seats, you may have to make up new seat mounting plates. Follow the same rules for size and thickness as described for seat belts.

Brackets and fittings

Various brackets and fittings exist under every car, and they are often overlooked when a repair is being made. For example a new section of floor may be welded in, but there may be no bracket to hold an exhaust pipe.

Above **A rear valance for this
early Ford Capri was only
available in fibreglass, so I
decided to make my own in
steel. This is the result. You
cannot see the joins at the
corner!**

Right **The other side of that
wheelarch. A whole new sheet of
steel has been welded in and
some work is still going on at
the bottom**

The simplest form of bracket is a small strip of steel about two to three inches long and $\frac{1}{2}$ an inch wide. The bracket is bent at the required angle and one end is then welded to the floor. The other end either has a hole in it, or a captive nut. This type of bracket is often used to mount brake pipes and cables. Similarly, more sturdy brackets are used to mount exhaust pipes and handbrake cables.

Brackets should be made by following the same procedure as for other parts. Mark out on paper, followed by card, the required shape. Then mark out the steel from the cardboard pattern. It is often easier to drill a hole in a bigger sheet of steel, so I suggest you drill the required holes before cutting out the bracket.

A small bracket like this is often difficult to secure in place prior to welding. Drill a small pilot hole through both the bracket and the floor panel where it is to be mounted. Then use a pop rivet to hold the bracket in place. Once it is in its final position, tack weld the bracket in place. Now drill out the pop rivet and plug the hole with a puddle weld.

Brackets like this can be made in fairly heavy gauge steel, perhaps 14 or 16 gauge. Once welded in place, they can be adjusted by bending.

Brackets which carry a heavy load must be made shorter and stronger. This type of bracket rarely rusts, so you can often salvage the original bracket from a piece of discarded floor section. This is another reason for not throwing away any scrap until the complete job is done.

Exhaust pipes are often held in place by thick rubber bands. These bands are held to hooks on the floor. Again, try to salvage the original hook from a scrap floor panel. Alternatively, make a new hook from a bolt, bent to the required shape and welded in position.

Brackets for bumpers are usually strongly made and often need only a good rub down with a wire brush and a repaint. Remember that where these brackets are mounted to the body, a ledge is often formed, and that this can trap dirt and begin the rusting process. Once the job is finished, treat these ledges with underseal.

Once you have renewed all the rusty chassis sections, why not replace the brake pipes? New copper pipes will not rust and a kit to suit most cars can be obtained from Handy

Brake Pipes, whose address appears at the end of the book.

These copper pipes are fastened to the chassis by neat little plastic clips. All you have to do is drill a $\frac{1}{4}$ in. hole and press one half of the clip into the hole. The other part of the clip holds the copper pipe. Press the two parts of the clip together and the pipe is firmly held.

Finally, mud flaps are often held by simple brackets which can easily be made from a piece of scrap steel, probably 14 or 16 gauge. Drill the holes before you cut out the bracket. It is best to model your new brackets on the old ones.

Rustproofing

After you have done all the restoration work, and your pride and joy has a sound chassis again, you will want to ensure that you do not have to light up the torch again for a

This Ford Motor Company drawing shows where sealer is applied around the floorpan/chassis areas

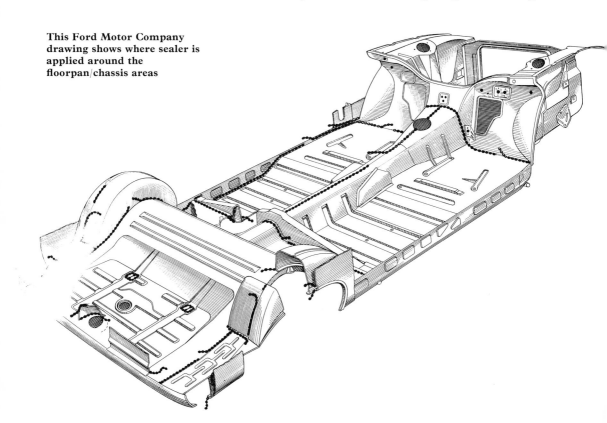

long time. There are many ways to protect the underside of a car. Basically they all aim to prevent water from coming into contact with bare metal.

The large flat areas of the floor pan will only give trouble if the carpets and underfelt get wet—in other words they will rust from the top, down. Think about that. On a flat sheet of steel there is nowhere for water to gather and cause rust, it just drips off.

The main problem areas are the box sections which you have patiently repaired. This is where mud and debris can build up. This material stores water, acting like a sponge, and this soon leads to rust.

If you intend to rustproof the whole of the car, first it pays to have the underside washed with a high pressure washer or steam cleaner. Many garages now have these on the forecourt and you can do the work yourself. All you need is to put the money into the slot and switch on.

Make sure you get all the mud, dirt and loose underseal off. Put the jet into all the awkward areas, such as under the wheelarches.

When you have done the cleaning, get some rags and mop up as much of the loose water from the underside of the car as you can. Some people take it for a short run to blow away excess water. But remember—make sure its a dry day!

Dry off each area before applying any rust fixers.

It is difficult to give general instructions about rust inhibitors. You will have to follow the instructions which come with the product. Generally they have quite clear instructions. Basically, what you have to do is clean off any loose paint, dirt or other debris. Paint on the rust inhibitor as described by the manufacturer. Sometimes you have to apply a second coat, while others have to be washed off with water. It pays to treat one small area at a time. Follow the instructions closely. When the rust proofer has cured for the required time, you can then paint on underseal or bitumen.

Underseal

There are several kinds of underseal. In any case, you have to remove all loose paint, dirt or old underseal so that the

Top **And here is just one of the many types of sealer on the market. Have a look round your local supplier and make your choice**

Above **Silicon brake fluid. Well, it is quite expensive, but as it says on the bottle, 'the most advanced brake and clutch fluid ever formulated'**

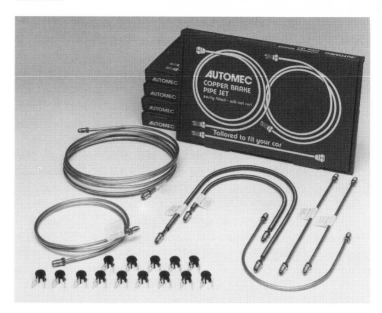

Right You would be well advised to fit a set of copper brake pipes. This finishes off your chassis restoration the best way

Below This is the tried and tested method of patching a chassis. The patch should only be welded top and bottom

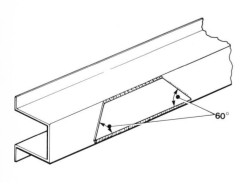

new underseal will bond tightly to the body. If you want to put on a second coat, do so, but allow the time for the first coat to dry. This will be marked on the tin.

Do not get underseal on the exhaust system. If you do, wipe it off at once with a cloth soaked in white spirit, paraffin or turpentine. The same solvents can be used to wipe any underseal from paintwork where it would show.

Now that the outside is rust inhibited and coated with a nice thick layer of underseal, what can you do to protect the insides of the box sections?

The manufacturers drill holes in the box sections to allow water and debris to drain out, but over the years these tend to block up, and the corrosion starts. The holes also allow the boxes to breathe, thus cutting down on damaging condensation.

These holes can be used to allow access to spray a rust inhibitor inside the box section. For this purpose, companies like Waxoyl provide an applicator tool which is small enough to go into these holes.

Get as much muck out of the box sections as you can. Poke it out with a welding rod or screwdriver, or—if you have the facilities—blow the muck out with compressed air. You must wear goggles if you do this, and keep everyone else well clear.

If you have been working on a box section you should have cleaned out as much muck as you could, while the box was open.

If you need to get in from above, then look for holes plugged with grommets, or even drill your own holes.

Left **Hammering one edge of a strip of steel like this produces a curve. This curved patch is useful at wheelarch corners, where the arch meets the boot floor**

Below **This is what happens when you finish welding but do not put some protective paint on. It rusts. Then you have to start cleaning off the rust with a grinder or wire brush**

IIO

CHASSIS

Once you have applied the rust treatment, plug the hole with a grommet. You will need about five litres to treat a small car, possibly double that for a bigger saloon, treble that for a US-sized machine.

When you have completed the rustproofing process and you are sure that no water is entering to form puddles on the floor, now is the time to lay some extra underfelt, to reduce noise levels. There are plenty of suppliers of underfelt, and they can also supply carpet and noise reduction kits. It all adds that little bit of comfort and refinement.

During your scrapyard visits don't forget to pick up some strips of compressed felt (sometimes known as 'filler') which is put in the grooves and channels of a typical floor panel. You will often find that filler from another car from the same maker will fit, if you cannot find the correct item. It is little things like this which make the difference between just a repair and a restoration to be proud of.

This Mini is having its front end rebuilt after an accident. The engine and subframe have been removed. Most of the metal work looks in good condition, rust-wise!

Draining sills

If you fit new sills it pays to make drain holes in them to prevent any further build up of rust. You could drill holes to act as a drain, but I prefer the following method.

If you have seam-welded the lower half of the sill, leave gaps of about half an inch, every nine inches or so. Get your $\frac{1}{4}$ in. screwdriver and tap it in between the inner and outer sill. When you get the blade in about $\frac{1}{4}$ in. twist the handle to force the two sheets of metal apart. If you repeat this process you will make slots, just like on the original sills. Every six months or so, just stick a welding rod into the slots to make sure they are clear of debris.

As has been mentioned before, I like to underseal the inner sill and the inside of the outer sill prior to welding, although I know that some of the underseal will be burnt off by the heat.

If the design of the car allows it, drill holes at either end of the sill which can be closed off with rubber bungs. Once a year you can then take the bungs out, unblock the sill and apply new rust inhibitor.

The subframe is in good condition, but it would be wise to clean it off thoroughly and apply some protective paint and underseal at this stage

Chapter 7 | How to gas weld

In this chapter, I want to try to tell you all the facts about gas welding that all the other books don't mention. However, I do not intend to cover aluminium welding. For the repair of car bodies and chassis there is no substitute for oxy-acetylene welding equipment. Many other systems have been developed and tried over the last few years, but for the amateur user *and* for sheer versatility nothing can equal gas.

With the introduction of British Oxygen's Portapac portable welding equipment in the UK, every British enthusiast with an interest in body repair can now own his personal welding set. You have much the best control with gas, and if you make a mistake, the worst you can do is burn a small hole. This can be filled in later.

By paying some £300 for the complete Portapac set, the home welder gets:

1. The rental of a small acetylene cylinder.
2. The rental of a small oxygen cylinder.
3. An acetylene regulator.
4. An oxygen regulator.
5. A welding torch.
6. A cutting torch attachment.
7. Three welding and two cutting tips or nozzles.
8. A length of special hose for oxygen, complete with all connections and emergency valves.
9. A length of special hose for acetylene, complete with all connections and emergency valves.
10. A cylinder key, multiple spanner for the connections and a smart trolley to contain all the equipment.
11. A selection of welding and brazing rods.
12. A pair of protective goggles.

Welding in a new floor patch. Note that the wiring loom is held up, well out of the way, and that the end of the welding wire has been bent over to prevent eye injuries when the goggles are taken off

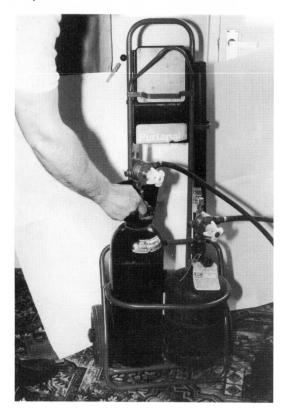

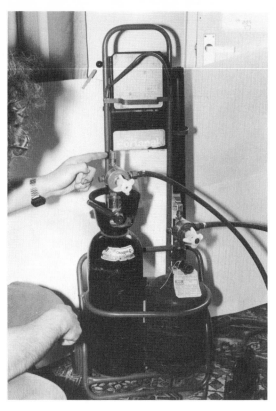

Above **Turn the gas on by using the spanner provided in the kit. Open slowly in the direction marked on the valve**

Right **When you have turned the bottles on, the amount of gas in each cylinder is registered on the gauge indicated. The Portapak cylinders will give you at least four hours solid welding**

13. A spark lighter for igniting the gas.
REMEMBER: these gas cylinders are *rented* from BOC so you cannot sell them. Each time you hand in an empty cylinder for a refill it is tested to ensure that it is still safe to use.

Refer to the handbook which comes with the equipment, and assemble the torch and hoses. Next check the size of the nozzle fitted to the welding torch. Normally, the smallest tip supplied will be a number 2. For bodywork you really want a number 1, but for chassis work a number 2 or 3 will be required. At this stage do not use anything bigger. (A new tip costs about £2, so is well worth buying a number 1 when you buy the Portapac).

If you wear glasses you will find that the goggles supplied are awkward to use. You should buy a set which also fit over spectacles. These are also available from BOC.

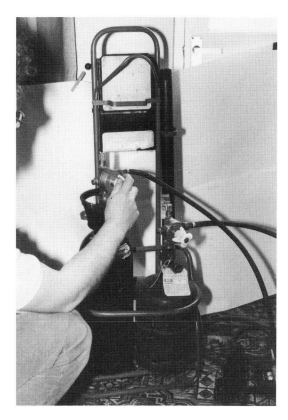

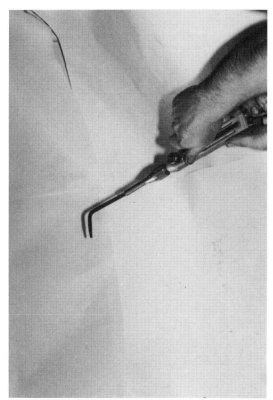

Before lighting the torch for the first time, make a final check that all connections are made properly. Remember that fittings for combustible gases (in our case acetylene) use left-handed threads to distinguish them, so bear this in mind when tightening connections.

Set the regulators on the bottles to 2 lb. Slowly turn on the bottles with the key provided. Put the protective goggles on. Always wear the goggles. You cannot weld properly without them. The flame burns at around 6300° F (3500° C) and the fierce brightness can cause temporary blindness if viewed directly. Gas welding is largely a matter of common sense, and wearing goggles is one of the 'musts'.

Turn the acetylene on at the torch, about one quarter turn. There should be a slight hiss of escaping gas. With the welding tip pointing towards the ground, spark the

Left **Adjust the gas pressure using the white knob on the front. Recommended pressures are around 2 lb per sq. in., but you might have to vary this from kit to kit**

Above **When all the bottles are turned on, and the pressures adjusted, you can turn on the torch and listen for gas. The acetylene has a distinctive smell. When lighting the torch, point it towards the ground**

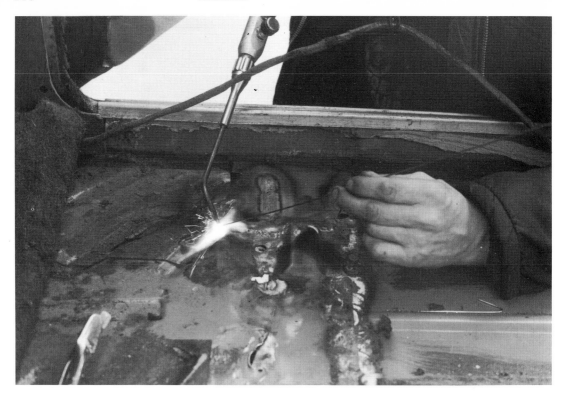

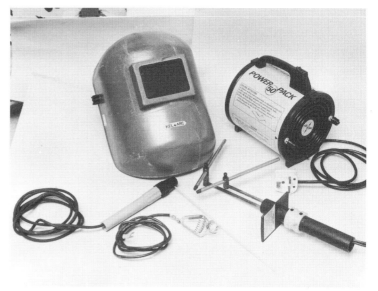

Above **Welding a patch in place. The tear in the foreground will be dressed with hammer and dolly and then welded**

Right **I often use this air-cooled electric welding set for plug welds. It has many other uses too, including a handy carbon arc torch**

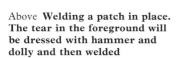

lighter about half an inch in front of the tip. The acetylene will light and burn with a bright yellow and very sooty flame. Next, turn on the oxygen very slowly and adjust the two control knobs on the torch until you have a flame which looks even. The flame will burn with an even sizzling sound. You now have what is known as a neutral flame. This is all very difficult to describe, but a few minutes with the equipment will make everything clear.

You might have to experiment with the regulator pressures a little as the pressures I have quoted are only for guidance. Once you have lit the torch, it is time for a little practice. If you have never welded before, it helps to think of the torch as a paint brush of which you have total control. With a properly adjusted flame you are painting the metal—first red, and then as the temperature increases, yellow.

Practice moving the torch across a piece of scrap steel. Now and again pause to heat a small area locally. Watch how the surface of the metal changes as the temperature increases. Next heat an area of the metal until you burn a hole. Repeat this, but this time do not let a hole burn through. Instead, just as you think a hole is about to develop, gently pull the tip back from the metal to reduce the heat. There is no way to describe what you are looking for. That is why you have to try it yourself on some scrap steel plate. If you judge it correctly, you will have avoided burning a hole while managing to heat the steel to melting point.

This is the trick in gas welding. Too many people, even very experienced and trained mechanics, make the mistake of not heating the metal enough. If they then apply filler rod, the result is a few lumps of filler rod stuck on the surface of the parent metal. This shows a poor understanding of the welding process, as well as producing a weak and potentially dangerous weld.

Having spent half an hour or so with the torch, you will now want to try to join two pieces of scrap metal together. Lay two pieces of scrap steel on two bricks with the edges of the steel about $\frac{1}{16}$ in. apart. (This is just the thickness of the welding rod). If you have bought clamps, then clamp the sheets the same distance apart. If you have a choice of

Two holes in the thinner sheet of steel, clamped in place and ready to be plug or puddle welded

tips, put in a number 1 or 2. Light the torch and put on your goggles. Adjust the flame as we described earlier. Make sure the flame is burning at the torch tip, not $\frac{1}{4}$ in. in front of the tip. If it is burning in front of the tip, the pressure is too high, so either turn the regulators down a little way, or adjust the flame with the controls on the torch.

Start to heat the metal. I will have to assume that you are right-handed, so if you are not, 'reverse' the hands in this description. Hold the torch in the right hand and about half way along the body of the torch. Do not grip it too tightly. Do *not* be afraid of it. It is just another tool which you are learning to use. Make sure that the hose is lying freely on the ground, rather than snagged under the trolley or some other obstruction. Take the filler rod in the left hand and hold it about six inches from its end. Bend over the last few inches of the opposite end, to prevent you sticking it in the lens of your goggles.

Move the tip of the torch slowly across both pieces of metal so that a small area on each side of the join is brought up to temperature. Try to keep the tip of the torch at about 60 degrees to the metal. This is the best angle which produces the neatest welds.

If you are going to tack the two pieces of metal together first, then concentrate the heat in a small area. When both pieces of steel are just starting to melt, bring the welding rod into the flame and heat it. If you get everything right, the two pieces of steel will form a puddle and the molten end of the filler rod can be introduced to the puddle. Fusion will then take place and you will be left with your first tack weld.

Don't give up if it does not work out first time. Try again. Remember, too much heat will blow a hole, too little heat will not give you a molten puddle. This is a difficult process to describe and I have not yet found a book which properly described what is happening. You have to try it. It's a bit like learning to swim on top of the kitchen table. Great for practice, but you do need water!

If you find the torch is backfiring, this is due to incorrect pressure, an overheated tip or loose tip, or allowing the tip to touch the work. When you have made a tack

Above **It looks worse than it is. The floor patch is in place and ready to be finished with the grinder. After a coat of primer and some underseal, it will look better than new**

Left **This is the part of the restoration which bothers me most. The screen pillar is made from three layers of steel. Here the outer layer is rusted through. What lies beneath?**

weld, shut off the acetylene, then the oxygen, in that order. Put the torch down in a safe place. Allow the steel to cool. If you are using clamps or have two pairs of pliers, try to break the tack weld. Chances are your first welds will break. What this means is either that they are too small, or more likely that you have not used enough heat and not achieved the correct penetration. The ideal situation is that the steel should bend before the tack weld breaks. If you can, get someone to show you how to weld. I learnt how to weld in one afternoon. I have been getting better ever since.

Because you will be working over your head, whether you have ramps or a pit, there are a number of extra dangers to be aware of.

Firstly, hot pieces of metal or spatter may fall on you. Protective clothing is essential but *do not* wear nylon trousers or overalls as burning metal can melt nylon with

Mid way through chiselling off the old sill. You can see the lips of the new outrigger ready to meet bright new steel

painful results. Overhead welding puts a terrific strain on
your arms and neck. You must have room to move about
and get comfortable. Do a small piece of work at a time,
then take a rest. You must work safely. You must be able to
reach the job from both sides, unless you can weld both
right- and left-handed. Keep all steel clean. Do not weld
over paint.

Always tack before welding. This gives you an extra
chance to correct any mistakes and helps prevent
distortion. Some authorities say you should tack weld, then
complete the job in one quick run. Others point out that
you should make short runs and allow the metal to cool
between runs. Both groups agree that the 'skip' method
(where you do a few inches then move away to weld another
area) is safer for the less experienced. Certainly this is the
way I work.

**The rusty part of the inner sill
has been cut away, and in this
shot you can see the first repair
part welded in**

Another view of the inner sill, this time from the inside. You can see where the welding line is and how the outrigger is welded to the inner sill. Once protected with paint and underseal, this repair should last a very long time

Plug welding

Although I do not think that you cannot successfully restore a car with an arc welder, there are occasions when one can be useful. The technique I am going to describe is known as either 'plug welding,' 'puddle welding' or even 'spot welding'. I prefer to call it plug welding.

Basically it consists of drilling a hole in one sheet of steel and welding through the hole to the other sheet. The joddler or joggling tool often has a punch which is ideal for creating holes for plug welding.

If you are welding a chassis outrigger onto a floor panel, you will drill or punch the holes in the floor. This process can save a lot of welding from underneath. It reduces distortion and is also very neat.

Having drilled the hole, clamp the two sheets of steel together. If you are using gas, melt the lower sheet of steel through the hole. Let some of the heat spread to the edges of the upper layer of steel. When the lower layer starts to puddle, feed in some filler rod and blend the two layers together, filling the hole at the same time. The technique needs a bit of practice to produce neat results. You must ensure that complete penetration has been achieved, which means that the lower layer of steel must be hot enough to melt. It is no use adding filler rod to stick to the top of the

lower sheet. It must all fuse in to achieve a sound weld.

You can use almost the same process with electric arc welding. Choose a size of electric welding rod which suits the size of the hole. Remember that the electric arc is very much hotter than gas (it's some 4000° C or 7000° F) so you have less time before the steel melts.

Having clamped the two sheets of steel together, connect the earth lead for the arc welder to the chassis. Put on the mask and protective gloves. Button up any open-necked shirts otherwise you will get a painful sunburn from the ultra-violet rays.

Strike the arc by either tapping the end on the steel, or by scratching it across the steel. In a very short time the steel, will start to melt, so you have to complete the plug weld quickly. You will have to practice on some scrap to find the best current setting for your repair. A circular motion of the welding electrode will also aid the plug welding process.

I recommend that you practice both techniques on scrap steel before you even lay hands on your car. If you decide to use plug welding, do not just go one, two, three along the seam. Skip from one hole to another to reduce the chances of distortion.

The great advantage of this process is that you do not

The outrigger, showing how it is welded to the old part of the chassis member. A small patch is required to join the new outrigger to the chassis member above the silencer box

have to lie on the ground. Enough closely grouped spot welds will provide plenty of strength. Being a 'belt and braces' man, I always go under the car anyway and gas weld in a few short seams after I have hammered in the lips close to the floor. (This helps stop water getting into the joint).

The biggest problem is drawing a line on the upper layer of steel, to line up with the lower layer.

Once you have completed a section of welding, use the hammer and dolly to 'dress' the welds. This means to flatten them. This makes the job neater but is also supposed to give extra strength to the weld.

Always keep both pieces of steel to be welded clean and paint-free. The heat of the torch will burn off paint, but there are two very good reasons for *not* doing this:

1. The extra heat will add to your distortion problems. Take my word for it. I was guilty of this for years, until it was pointed out to me.
2. Fumes are given off when you burn paint. It is unpleasant, dirty and dangerous.

The following is a list of DOs and DON'Ts for welders. Pay close attention to them. They will all help improve your technique:

DO NOT light the torch with both valves open.

ALWAYS shut off the acetylene valve on the torch first.

Keep the welding flame AWAY FROM THE HOSES.

CLOSE the cylinders when not in use. This means when you go for lunch, as well as at the end of the working day.

SEARCH for leaks, *only* with soapy water.

KEEP the torch moving to avoid blowing holes. Zig-zag if necessary.

START from the right-hand side of the job and work towards the left (this assumes the torch is in your right hand).

KEEP the nozzle angle at 60–70° relative to the work.

ALWAYS use a neutral flame for all mild steel welding.

ALWAYS weld with the apex or outer extremes of the white cone in the flame.

ALWAYS put the extra heat on the thicker steel.

HEAT only enough to weld. *Do not* try to burn off paint.

ALWAYS weld clean steel.

Appendix

Useful addresses

Practical Classics and *The Automobile*
5 Rectory Road,
Beckenham,
Kent,
BR3 1HL

Practical Classics is the ideal magazine for the older-car owner and enthusiast. Published monthly.
The Automobile is for veteran, vintage and pre-1940s cars and commercial vehicle owners and enthusiasts. Published monthly.

Automec Equipment and Parts Ltd,
Arden House,
West Street,
Leighton Buzzard,
Bedfordshire,
LU7 7DD

Suppliers of copper Handy Brake Pipes, clutch and fuel pipe sets tested to 10,000 lbs, and silicone brake fluid.

A T A Engineering Processes,
Ebberns Road,
Hemel Hempstead,
Herts.

Suppliers of a wide range of temporary fasteners including the plier-operated rivet clamps often known as Cleco Clamps.

P S W Panels Coventry,
76A Albany Road,
Earlsdon,
Coventry,
CV5 6JU
West Midlands

Replacement motor panel specialists.

A P D Body Panels Ltd,
Unit 22,
Aston Church Trading Estate,
Aston Church Road,
Nechells,
Birmingham

Wide range of top quality, guaranteed body panels and repair sections for British and foreign cars.

L M C Panels,
Quartermaster Road,
West Wilts Trading Estate,
Westbury,
Wiltshire,
BA13 4JT

Large selection of replacement body panels and steel pressings for British and foreign cars.

Pop-On Body Spares Ltd,
Skeldon,
Hollybush,
by Ayr,
Scotland,
KA6 7EB

Specialists in manufacture and supply of high quality car body and chassis repair panels.

Peter Rhodes,
Tanshelf Industrial Estate,
Pontefract,
West Yorkshire.

Wide selection of body and chassis repair parts.

British Oxygen Company (BOC)
See address of local sales depot in telephone directory.

Suppliers of industrial welding gases and equipment.
Suppliers of Portapak equipment.

Index